*Almost There* reads like a long-awaited letter from a long-lost friend. It's immersive, as the best kind of storytelling should be. It's honest and warm, as the best kinds of friends are. DiFelice writes about home as it's lived and lost and loved. Her book is a rewarding read!

**JEN POLLOCK MICHEL**
Author of *Teach Us to Want: Longing, Ambition, and the Life of Faith* and *Keeping Place: Reflections on the Meaning of Home*

If you've ever left something behind, you'll find a friend in Bekah DiFelice as she invites you on a quest to find home. Bekah shares her adventures (and misadventures), helping us all discover that even transplanted roots can go deep.

**CATHERINE McNIEL**
Author of *Long Days of Small Things: Motherhood as a Spiritual Discipline*

Among the stories and thoughts that Bekah DiFelice shares in her debut book are her joyful passion and earnest quest to live life fully. *Almost There* is packed with so many relatable themes, including fear, longing, doubt, and identity. Bekah's story will not only help you discover big and small pieces of your own story but will also encourage and inspire you to pursue your own new adventures, wherever you are. A beautiful storyteller whose heart for God and family shines, Bekah gives us all a gift of light and love in *Almost There*.

**JESSICA N. TURNER**
*Wall Street Journal* bestselling author of *The Fringe Hours: Making Time for You*

"Are we there yet?" No, not until you pick up this book and start reading. I expected to skim through these pages, on the way to somewhere else. I had to stop. And laugh. And savor. And wonder. This is a trip I hope many take, because Bekah DiFelice brilliantly shows us where to finally hang our hats—and our hearts.

**LESLIE LEYLAND FIELDS**
Author of *Crossing the Waters: Following Jesus through the Storms, the Fish, the Doubt, and the Seas*

Bekah DiFelice writes beautifully and profoundly about our longing for and journey toward a true sense of home. This book is for all who are yearning for a belonging deeper than this world can offer. When I read the middle sections of *Almost There*, I was at that time overwhelmed by a family crisis and was feeling desperate, orphaned, and lost. Bekah's chapters on fear and on faith and doubt reached out to my brokenness . . . and I began to stumble back to my true home where my Abba was waiting with his secure love. Wherever you are in your pilgrimage, *Almost There* will meet you and embrace you, and it will provide intimate, heartfelt companionship for the rest of your journey.

**J. KEVIN BUTCHER**
Author of *Choose and Choose Again: The Brave Act of Returning to God's Love*

Our path to maturity in Christ is often accelerated when we find ourselves dealing with change that is thrust upon us rather than chosen. Through the lens of military life, and with animated style, young wife Bekah chronicles life on the move for herself and her husband, Mike. With her captivating take on the unexpected elements she found embedded in marriage, moving, injury, deployment, and pregnancy, Bekah enlists us to share in her inmost responses of faith. Her story is an enjoyable read that touches the deep places of faith many young women experience.

**DANA YEAKLEY**
Author of *The Gentle Art of Discipling Women: Nurturing Authentic Faith in Ourselves and Others*

*Searching for Home
in a Life on the Move*

Bekah DiFelice

ALMOST

THERE

NAVPRESS ✺

A NavPress resource published in alliance
with Tyndale House Publishers, Inc.

NavPress is the publishing ministry of The Navigators, an international Christian organization and leader in personal spiritual development. NavPress is committed to helping people grow spiritually and enjoy lives of meaning and hope through personal and group resources that are biblically rooted, culturally relevant, and highly practical.

**For more information, visit www.NavPress.com.**

*Almost There: Searching for Home in a Life on the Move*

Copyright © 2017 by Bekah DiFelice. All rights reserved.

A NavPress resource published in alliance with Tyndale House Publishers, Inc.

*NAVPRESS* and the NAVPRESS logo are registered trademarks of NavPress, The Navigators, Colorado Springs, CO. *TYNDALE* is a registered trademark of Tyndale House Publishers, Inc. Absence of ® in connection with marks of NavPress or other parties does not indicate an absence of registration of those marks.

The Team:
Don Pape, Publisher
Caitlyn Carlson, Acquisitions Editor
David Zimmerman, Copyeditor
Nicole Grimes, Designer

Cover photograph of car copyright © by Cristian Lupu/Getty Images. All rights reserved.

Cover photograph of field copyright © by Johner Images/Getty Images. All rights reserved.

Author photo by Brent Austin, copyright © 2015. All rights reserved.

Some of the anecdotal illustrations in this book are true to life and are included with the permission of the persons involved. All other illustrations are composites of real situations, and any resemblance to people living or dead is purely coincidental.

Fo information about special discounts for bulk purchases, please contact Tyndale House Publishers at csresponse@tyndale.com or call 1-800-323-9400.

Cataloging-in-Publication Data is available.

ISBN 978-1-63146-471-3

Printed in the United States of America

| 23 | 22 | 21 | 20 | 19 | 18 | 17 |
|----|----|----|----|----|----|----|
| 7  | 6  | 5  | 4  | 3  | 2  | 1  |

*For my neighborhood and the transient military community within, especially the fellow moms who congregated at the park with me every afternoon.*

*By the time you read this, we will have moved away, which seems appropriate, somehow. May you discover the richness of home in every place you are and find friends that become family as you were to us for the brief time our addresses aligned.*

# CONTENTS

# ADRIFT

For most of my life I have wondered if I belonged somewhere else. I imagined that alternative versions of myself
existed in places I hadn't yet been, that unknown lands
were the key to self-improvement, enhanced social skills,
and better skin. From the vantage point of my hometown,
I thought that if I could just linger in a foreign country—
you know, develop an accent or climb the right mountain
or stumble into the right place at the right time—I might
encounter the best-case scenario of my life. I thought that
if I could get to the right location, I would finally arrive
where I belong.

This sensation of belonging is what I've come to think
of as home—a feeling of being inwardly settled, as if your
soul gets to sink into a couch with deep cushions after a
long day of being on its feet. Each of us has a deeply personal concept of home. It's an intimate place by nature,
and often one difficult to describe. *Home* tends to grow
in explanation and complexity over time, sort of like fine

cheese or, say, the weight you have listed on your driver's license.

Originally, home is your parents' house, the place you grow up, where you store your old porcelain dolls or the Field Day ribbons that represent your crowning achievement of the fourth grade. Home is where you boomerang back to at the end of each day to do homework or eat dinner or sprint up the steps to make curfew by the slimmest margin. It's where you are called by a mortifying nickname, where your stocking hangs at Christmas, where a framed family photo immortalizes your unfortunate hair-crimping phase. For however brief a time, home is a fixed address, a single location.

But then there is a shift, a change, a disrupting curiosity. The timing is different for everyone—perhaps in childhood or during high school or when you read a novel that transports you into a different kingdom. But it happens: Your sense of belonging outgrows its previous residence. You suspect you need a fresh start—different friends, a different opportunity. You need to live away from family, to chart your own path, to get your own place. Home, then, becomes a quest driven by the belief that peace and rest are out there somewhere, if only you could find them on a map or in a career field or among a community of people who finally "get you." In the search for home, we all try on different places and relationships and hobbies like outfits that make us feel pretty, all along lamenting the fact that belonging refuses to be nailed down to exact coordinates. It denies us permanence. And that feels like betrayal.

I think that by nature we are agitated by this restlessness, by the enigma of belonging. We're pestered by the notion that people and places and things are all important pieces of home but not the whole thing, at least not in themselves. Deep down we know there is a permanence of home that exists somewhere. There is a whisper of eternity that beckons in the heart of every one of us.[1] So it seems, almost by necessity, that home must expand beyond its physical definition and broaden into a more spiritual one. This, I think, is when the real search for home begins, when we look for *Home* in its singular, uppercase form, when we pursue it as a permanent destination, an orienting landmark amid the impermanence of everything else.

I don't presume this is the case for everyone, but in my experience the pursuit of home has been a pursuit of God—because I need to know that peace and rest can be found in every place I am, that there is reason and rightness beneath the chaos of my days. I need a spiritual home so that when former iterations of home expire, I'm still assured that a deeper belonging holds fast. I need a Home that ministers to me the same way the tug and pull of an anchor murmurs solace to a ship: *Take heart, restless one. You aren't adrift after all.*

# CHAPTER ONE

# GILA BEND
## On Leaving Home

*Home is where one starts from.*

T. S. ELIOT, "East Coker"

It was in the desert that I realized I was far from home.

I sat on the curb of a small-town gas station, listening to the buzz of a failing fluorescent lightbulb and the hiss of cars passing by. It was late. Close to midnight, I think. The desert sun had long descended into darkness, but it was still hot. One hundred and twelve degrees hot. And I'm going to be honest with you—the back sweat situation was widespread and alarming. I pulled my shirt away from my perspiring torso like gum from a shoe.

I was in Gila Bend, Arizona. "Home to 1,700 Friendly People and 5 Old Crabs," according to the whitewashed sign near the highway. Inside the convenience store was an array of souvenirs ranging from fermented rattlesnake and porcelain cacti to an entire aisle of creepy-crawly knickknacks that would thrill a nine-year-old boy. Hot dogs were two for a dollar and cigarettes were on sale and Mexico was only eighty miles away.

Our bright yellow moving truck was parked nearby, speckled with kamikaze bugs smeared across the windshield. I had followed my husband here, and that husband had followed the Marine Corps here, obeying his first set of military orders all the way to the outer fringes of Arizona, the sunbaked miles of almost-Mexico. He was being stationed in Yuma, Arizona, at a small air station ten miles from the border.

Do you know where Yuma is?

Yeah, I didn't either.

Our engagement was spent on the phone, as Mike trained in Quantico and I finished college in Colorado. When it came time to wait on military orders, Mike spoke confidently about the options. He said that San Diego was likely where we would be stationed—that's what he requested, after all—although Hawaii or Japan were possibilities as well. Since we had not yet lived under the discretion of the military, Mike and I mistakenly assumed that the military would cooperate with our best-laid plans, that perhaps it would consult our thoughts and feelings before making arbitrary decisions about our future, as though it were a waitress taking our order and offering helpful suggestions before ultimately giving us what we wanted.

For the record, the military is not at all like a waitress. It's more like a cafeteria lady—a domineering force with hair netting, bushy eyebrows, and heavily perspiring forehead—scowling at you from behind a cloudy sneeze guard. She puts on your tray whatever's available, whatever she likes, a menu predetermined in high-up, unseen places. And your job is to say thank you, to make the most of it. Your job is to keep moving.

But Mike and I didn't know this yet. We were just a couple of twenty-two-year-olds, idealistic and hungry for adventure. So in the waiting period of engagement, Mike and I discussed the luxury of living near an ocean, the possibility of learning how to surf, the prospect of living in Asia. I told my girlfriends about these exotic locations while twirling my engagement ring and awkwardly pronouncing the word *fiancé*.

Mike's orders came on a Friday afternoon in November. He had been in the field for the past two weeks mastering skills of land navigation, which basically meant he was learning how to use a compass while wearing camouflaged face paint as I waited for him to call. When he finally did, I was quick to answer.

"Hello?"

"Hi," he answered. "I got orders." His voice sounded quiet, calculated.

"What? Where?" I demanded.

"Arizona." The verdict sounded rehearsed, as if he had practiced it over and over again, rolling it around his tongue and speaking it aloud until the word drained itself of emotion.

Somehow I could sense the aftertaste of disappointment on his tongue, the discouragement he was trying to conceal. Somehow I knew that it was bad news he was trying to spin into good.

"Arizona." I repeated it aloud. First as a statement. Then as a question. My eyes darted side to side as I took a mental inventory of everything I knew about Arizona: Phoenix, golf courses, cacti, rattlesnakes, suntans, retirees, prescription deodorant.

"I can do Arizona," I said, more to convince myself than him. "Where in Arizona?"

Silence.

I heard him breathing, procrastinating.

One second.

Two seconds. Three. Four.

The silence sounded distinctly like dread.

"Where in Arizona?" I prompted.

He used to do this. He still does this. Mike takes an enormous amount of time to break big news. He is a careful decision maker, thoughtful and impossibly thorough. I'm certain that he organizes his thoughts before thinking them, aligning them squarely to one side and alphabetizing them when time allows. He reveals a decision slowly, feeding details one by one and waiting for me to chew, swallow, and digest before giving me more.

"MIKE. Where?" I yelled into the phone.

"Yuma," he whispered.

One word. No context. Mike delivered the news reluctantly, driving it like a flag into the space between us. We both stared at it in the distance as it waved frantic and final against a cloudless sky.

Yuma. For three years.

I opened my laptop and searched "Yuma, Arizona," frantically skimming the top results: Sunniest place on earth. Hottest city in America. Home of Yuma Territorial Prison.

Sun. Heat. Prison.

*Sun. Heat. Prison.*

SUN! HEAT! PRISON!

It was late fall in Colorado when I absorbed these words. The notion of Yuma arrived while I was wearing a sweater and wool socks, while I was sitting on a twin bed cloaked in flannel sheets and a down comforter. I owned nine jackets at the time and only one pair of flip-flops. The flip-flops were incidental leftovers from summer camp. I called them "shower shoes."

Colorado was home to me because it was where I grew up. The outdoorsy, casual persona had been nurtured into me, and I was proud of it. Mountains were my everyday companions, tall chaperones that waited outside all ordinary places: grocery stores and gas

stations and suburban backyards. My lungs had a sense
of athletic superiority because I grew up at high altitude.
"Sea level" was a term you used to feel sorry for people
who lived near natural disasters.

Yuma was at sea level. And when ranked alphabeti-
cally, it was basically last. *Did that matter?* I wondered.

*Sun. Heat. Prison.* I turned the words over and over.

"Wait," I said to Mike with growing panic, "you are
moving me away from home. To the hottest place on
earth. To live among criminals?"

Silence.

*"Do you realize that is the actual definition of hell?"*

Mike and I dated for six years before we got engaged. We
were high school sweethearts, so, you know, *adorable.*
Yuma was our new task, our first joint assignment away
from home. So I suppose I should have felt a swelling
sense of destiny and purpose and excitement. But those
feelings didn't come until later. They came slowly, over
weeks and months. To this day, I don't really know how
a person adapts to change. But I suspect that most of the
time you just have to live into it, to take deep breaths
and get out of bed in the morning and trust that inter-
ruption usually doubles as provision, even when you
can't see the how or why yet.

When I look back at the time between that phone
call and the day I moved away, I don't recall a moment

of breakthrough or epiphany, a moment when I came to terms with the unexpectedness of Yuma as my temporary home. I do remember a lot of emotional eating and Google research on whether rattlesnake repellent was a thing. It's not, in case you're wondering, which is why I told Mike that I'd prefer to live on the second story of a secure fortress if we had to live in the desert. He laughed as if I were joking.

I was not.

Over and over again I told friends and family about our orders, saying no, Mike didn't request Yuma . . . no, we didn't even know it was an option . . . and yes, we were getting excited . . . sort of. Passing days wore down the shock of the news until our excitement became meager, fragile, then eventually real. Arizona wasn't so far from Colorado. We heard that there was hiking and recreation on the Colorado River. "Outdoorsy people love it!" a non-outdoorsy person once told us. We heard, too, that a small town was a good place to build meaningful relationships, which was absolutely true. Perspective arrived for us day by day until the location became a small footnote on the bigger announcement: Mike and I were getting married. And we were moving to a place of our own.

At least in my experience, I've found that pressing into big change doesn't always translate into easy or instant enthusiasm. Even good surprises tend to knock the wind right out of you. They often feel more like an invasion, a redirection, a total inconvenience. Adapting to change is like tucking your knees in when somebody wants to squeeze by your seat, or hitting the brakes for a car to merge ahead of you when you're already in a hurry. Adapting to change is making room for something you didn't expect in space that's already crowded. For most of us, it is painful and annoying.

Resilience, then, is a trait that has to be stretched—or shocked—into us. It's the prize of those who have watched their placeholders of control crumble and have lived to see how there was, in fact, a future beyond the circumstance that they considered the end of the world. For all the ways Yuma was not at all what I wanted, it was in many ways exactly what I needed. Does that sound trite? Perhaps it is. But even though the move was not preceded by excitement, it was eventually followed by a deep sense of gratitude. And I think this is true of a lot of change. We can experience the vast potential of what's next only after we are forced to step away from what came before.

I'm not sure I would have ever left Colorado on my own. I would have talked about it and planned it and made excuses to stay while meaning to go. I would have grown swollen with potential but remained fixed to the comforts of home. I'm not sure I would have ever uprooted if I'd had to do it alone. I'm a tiny bit bold, but mostly

I'm impulsive, reckless, and unbelievably bad at packing. This is why God linked me up with a responsible
Marine, I think. Mike did not rescue me, but his companionship did make me braver and better in every way.
And I loved him with such abandon that I would have
followed him anywhere.

So I did.

Just after our honeymoon and the day before we
moved, Mike and I decided to buy furniture since
we owned exactly none. On a Saturday afternoon we
pulled into a discount furniture store and purchased
items I assumed all adults owned: a sectional sofa, coffee table, and dining set. The two of us reclined side by
side on showroom sofas, sat in chairs that weren't ours,
and shared opinions that we made up on the spot: "Of
course I prefer microsuede!"

After an hour of canvassing the showroom floor,
Mike pulled the yellow moving truck around the back
of the store and asked the employees to load our newly
purchased furniture next to our newly received wedding gifts. It was all so tidy, the boxes on boxes that were
prelabeled and as geometrically compatible as a winning
game of Tetris. It felt like an accomplishment, that truck
that held our whole mobile life wrapped tight in plastic
and potential.

Preparing to leave might be the most thrilling part.
Still cushioned with the familiarity of home, you can
change your name and register for an absentee ballot

and purchase furniture for rooms that haven't felt resoundingly empty yet. There are a multitude of ways to say good-bye that require only an efficient execution of a checklist. And in the midst of change it's such a relief to have something to do, to have tasks that combat emotional pressure with endorphins of productivity. Before pulling out of the driveway, you can sprint through a dozen rites of passage in front of a cheering audience, fueled by excitement and home-cooked meals made by your mom.

The hard part for me was not the preparation. It was the actual leaving, the ducked head and enthusiastic wave down the backward descent of the driveway. It was saying good-bye without knowing if I would ever raise kids near my sister, if I would miss out on family milestones or holidays or lose touch with friends whom I considered lifelong. It was the fact that I had no idea what was coming. I had never been to Yuma, nor could I picture it at all. But I could see what I was leaving, what had been home most of my life. I knew Colorado. And it was in me, around me. So leaving it was a risk. It was giving up what I knew to gain what I didn't.

There's no guarantee that leaving and arriving are a fair trade. And this is nerve-racking, like painting a statement wall in the center of your living room or ordering beef lo mein at a restaurant without a safety rating. You have a hunch that this choice might improve or enhance your life, but in the end you're not totally sure how it's going to turn out. So you stand in your living room staring at the walls, or in the lobby of a restaurant looking at a menu with pixelated entrée photos, and in the end you decide whether or not you're the sort of person who's willing to risk, which is really another way of deciphering whether or not you're the sort of person willing to fail spectacularly.

At least for me, this is the hard part. Paint to wall. Fork to mouth. Car to road. The hard part is leaning into the risk and convincing yourself it's worth it. The hard part is finally, ultimately moving away from home. It is leaving. It is the uneasy silence that settles into the car after you merge onto the highway. Or if you can't bear the weight of silence, it is the song you turn on that will forever act as the soundtrack of this moment.

We left Colorado early in the morning, before the sun cracked light on the purple mountains. It seemed appropriate that this new endeavor coincided with the sunrise, like God was shining a flashlight pointing us west.

It takes fifteen hours to drive from Colorado Springs to Yuma, longer if you're following a rented moving truck that sways clumsily in the desert wind. My mom called every half hour while I squinted through the windshield and watched mountains give way to plains and plains succumb to desert. Soon the landscape was populated with plants sharpened slim as knives. Barbed wire grew out of cacti. The terrain was impossibly, insistently flat, a single plain that stretched for eternity.

When night set in, headlights flashed bright and aggressive from the opposite direction. So many people, it seemed, were fleeing from the very place I was headed. I departed Colorado armed with Cheez-Its and gusto, and in the desert I realized that both were gone. I started to feel a bit sad and homesick—mostly, I think, because I was tired, a symptom that tends to light up the rest of my emotional circuit board.

There was so much hope and optimism for the next chapter. Of course there was. But still it was quite sad to mourn the end of something, to realize that a part of you is shrinking in the rearview mirror, and that when you wake up in the morning, your life will look completely different.

Practically speaking, I know that leaving home has a lot of reasonable advantages. It matures everyday humans into respectable citizens by making them independent and self-reliant. It trains them in building community, forces them to manage time and money and refrigerator inventory well. Away from home, we realize that cable television is, in fact, quite expensive, and that bills come at the unfair pace of once a month. Living in an unfamiliar space frightens us into the habit of locking the front door behind us. It also thrills us with the liberty to stock a freezer with ice cream or to vacuum without pants on.

To leave home is also to make room in an important interior way. It removes your associations, your affiliations, the characteristics and comforts of homes that came before. It is terrifying and exciting to arrive at a place where no one knows you, where suddenly it doesn't matter if you got good grades in high school or used to be a few pounds lighter or had a season where you were, regrettably, brunette. Suddenly you are no longer defined by your history or decisions, nor by the people who spoke into your future with plans that didn't match your own. The moment of departure is the moment of reinvention, of renewal, of freedom. The moment you get a redo on the adjectives associated with your name.

Isn't it interesting, then, that many of the famous people in the Bible had to first leave their homes before their real stories began? Abraham was called to leave his country before he knew where he was going. The Israelites were sent to the enormous waiting room of the desert before arriving in the Promised Land. Jesus collected disciples by first calling them off their fishing boats and into his companionship. All of these people were commissioned upon departure—to be the father of the faith, God's own special possession, fishers of men. They got big, important jobs. More than that, though, they were christened with adjectives like *chosen* and *beloved*. They received promises of God's faithfulness directly, persistently, and in one case, in the form of manna. God became personal, relevant: a shepherd who leads from among, not a deity who exists absently from above.

It's as if the act of leaving is part of the equipping, as if God personally leads people out of familiar territory so he can tell them who they are.

Here's the thing about Gila Bend: It was the first place I realized I wasn't sure where my home was. I knew it was behind me in Colorado. And it was ahead of me also. Surely it had something to do with the ring around my finger now, this marriage, this man, and the mission we now had together. So, too, I knew home had something to do with the leading of a God who sends at the same time he receives, who gives my life purpose.[2] I knew that God was building a continuity of home within me somehow. I just didn't know how it all worked together. I still don't know how it works, really. But I suppose a desert is as good a place as any to get to the bottom of what you believe. To wring out what is true from the place where you're most desperate to see it: in the absence of the familiar, in the middle of the disruption.

While visiting Sequoia National Park several years ago, I read about how the enormous sequoia trees grow. There's a sign on one of the walking trails that tells the story of how one of the largest trees in the park fell down. A tragic collapse, one might say. Soon, though, the broken roots exposed bare soil in a sunny spot, creating the perfect conditions for a new tree to grow. And eventually a new tree did grow, a small but earnest sequoia that's still growing today. That spot is now marked by a sign that evangelizes the benefits of disruption to everyone who walks by on the footpath. "Disturbance is good for the environment," it reads. When I saw the sign, I felt a surge of hope. I took it as an indication of God's redemptive work in the world, regenerating the old into new, cultivating growth out of costly beginnings. The park named the site "Inheritance."

But when I think of inheritance, I don't think of disruption. I think of lushness and wealth, bounty and provision. The desert seemed to be the opposite of those things: severe and barren, the site of ruin rather than riches. As I sat on the curb in Gila Bend, I wondered: Could a desert be a good inheritance? Because that is what I had been given.

When Mike came out of the convenience store, he was armed with snacks. He offered me Skittles and I looked at him horrified, as if he didn't know me at all. To be fair, Mike didn't yet know how offended I am by desserts that are nonchocolate, by fruit charading as junk food. But at that moment he learned.

For a minute the two of us sat there together on the

curb, our knees cramped to chests, staring at the cars passing by while we ate pretzels, the bag loudly rustling beneath our fingers. We only had a couple of hours left on the drive, and then we'd be in Yuma. We'd be *home*. Is that what we'd call it?

In a single day we had driven from Colorado to Arizona: a small thing, I suppose. I mean, what did it involve, really? A handful of gas stops, bathroom breaks, and a half-finished book on tape? But it cost more, so much more, and sometimes you have to sit down and take it all in, the enormity of packing a car and a truck and pointing them away from home, as if by declaration.

On that curb, the magnitude of the day sank in. And we let it. Our silent fear and enormous hope for the future intermingled with each other until they became a single entity, a heavy, pulsing possibility laid upon our backs—or maybe it was a hand that gently urged us forward, onward, as if there were no other option, as if this were somehow an act of obedience, as if the new life we longed for were provided as a pathway directly through this wilderness.[3]

Perhaps that's what it feels like to be a tree giving way, or a seedling piercing through the ground.

Perhaps this is what it feels like to travel toward inheritance.

# CHAPTER TWO

# EMPTY ROOMS

## On Moving In

What is history? An echo of the past in the future;
a reflex from the future on the past.

VICTOR HUGO, The Man Who Laughs

Our first house was a two-story duplex that was an exact
replica of every other house on the street. I frequently
pulled into the wrong driveway. Just as frequently, neighbors pulled into mine.

Mike and I moved into base housing in Yuma on a
Saturday morning in June. There wasn't a cloud in the sky
or a breeze in the air to soften the ninety-degree temperature that met us first thing in the morning. Mike backed
the yellow moving truck into the driveway, slowly inching
his way toward the garage door. The engine roared in fits
and spurts while I waved my hands like an air traffic con-
troller: "A little bit more . . . a little bit more . . . a little bit
. . . STOP!"

Our front yard had jagged rocks instead of grass, rocks that matched the tan stucco of the house's exterior, as if the design inspiration for the neighborhood were drawn from the neutral, reptilian features of the lizards that darted through the yard.

Everything in the interior of that house was white: countertops, doors, floor tiles, and ceiling fans. The house was so sanitized, so empty. To say we moved into a blank slate, as clichéd as it is, is the truest description. The whole house was a whiteboard freshly erased of its previous tenants, saturated in bleach and paint primer to prepare for us, the temporary tenants. Because in military housing there really is no other kind of resident. We are all living in the neighborhood briefly, on military orders that generally stretch only two or three years. It's long enough to arrange the furniture, but generally not long enough to go to the trouble of painting the white walls.

The air-conditioning was already gusting through the house when we opened the front door. Mike didn't carry me across the threshold, as is the tradition for newlyweds, mostly because next to my fear of snakes and irregular textures in fruit-flavored yogurt is my severe aversion to cheesy romantic gestures. Even while eating fondue, I quite prefer to feed myself. So instead, the two of us carried couches, bed frames, and box springs through the garage and up the stairs into a house that smelled like industrial cleaning products.

Our footsteps clanged down the metal ramp of the truck, then whispered across the newly cleaned carpets as we stuttered step for step to carry a top-heavy dresser with taped-down drawers.

The military would have paid for movers to move us. I thought about this fact as Mike and I shuffled through narrow doorframes, him saying, "Watch your fingers! Watch your fingers!" and me saying, "It's slipping! It's slipping!" I thought about it as we rested midway up the stairs, propping between us a queen-size mattress that I can only assume was filled with liquid concrete or wet sand. I thought about it the following day when I became so dehydrated from moving furniture in triple-digit heat that I spent my second night in our new city at urgent care for a UTI.

It's funny, isn't it? Not the UTI, of course. The fact that doing hard things is often so entirely *optional*.

The incentive for us wasn't the fact that we could pocket the money the Marine Corps would have otherwise paid a moving company. It certainly wasn't for a sense of control over our precious clearance furniture. No, our trophy was a little sentence we have said over and over, both that day and long afterward.

*We moved ourselves.*

Perhaps this isn't true for everyone, but for us the act of moving wasn't just a change of address or change in scenery. It was an act of emancipation, a declaration of independence. We moved *ourselves* to make a point.

The point, of course, was that we were hard knocks. Legitimate adults. Fearless adventurers. I mean, look at this mattress I carried up the stairs. Look at these chairs I assembled with a miniature Allen wrench. Look at how painful it is to pee.

Late in the afternoon on that first day we sat on the white tile and leaned against the white walls and ate Domino's pizza. Mike and I sighed with satisfaction that, yes, we were finally living the grown-up version of our lives, specifically the part where we sat on the floor in a new, empty house, eating pizza straight from a box.

But even with all this glorious independence, there was a piece of me that had imagined that when I got married and moved into a new house, my mom or sister or any one of my best girlfriends would be there on opening day to help unpack boxes and offer suggestions on the most natural place to store a vacuum. Or I assumed, based on hearsay, that the military was so close in nature that friendly neighbors would be waiting at the door to offer brownies and casseroles and instant, sincere friendship. At least for us, that didn't happen. It was quiet on our street that day, too hot for kids to be playing in the street, the sun too aggressive for anyone to wash a car in the driveway without the soap drying to the paint. And in the desert, there were no humming lawn mowers, even on a Saturday, because there were no lawns to be mowed.

So Mike and I arrived in Yuma rather discreetly, without any fanfare or applause. This shouldn't have been a surprise, really, yet it was to me. There were no witnesses to the two of us unlocking the door to our first house, writing our name on the mailbox, or putting a welcome mat outside the front door. I'm not saying this is a tragedy. I'm just saying that sometimes doing a brave thing is more private than you expected it to be.

Of all the rooms in the house to unpack, the kitchen has to be the worst, don't you think? There are so many redundant dishes, all wrapped individually because they are fragile. One by one you unroll towels from around plates and newspaper from the insides of glasses or maybe taped-down bubble wrap if you're fancy. Then there is the putting away. The tedious, eternal putting away. The wondering why you do not currently own a utensil organizer or paper towel holder, such forgettable, essential things. What you do have, though, are ten identical forks, two dozen short and tall water glasses, and fourteen plastic Penn State cups your husband brought with him from across the country. In the kitchen, it seems you have either a dozen replicas of the same thing or none of them at all.

I began unpacking in the kitchen because my mom told me that this is the place to start. She said, "First you pull out dishes you can eat off of, and then you make sure there are sheets on a mattress you can sleep on at night." So when I didn't really know where to begin in our brand-new life, I found the box marked "Dishes/ Utensils/Shoes/Towels/Misc" and began unpacking, hoping I was better at kitchen organization than box categorization.

The newsprint stuffed around plates and inside glasses featured two-week-old stories from my hometown. As I unpacked, I read about the high school swimmer contending for a state championship and the construction project causing traffic delays on the highway. I saw a thumbnail picture of a sports columnist and realized I went to high school with his daughter. And I read that temperatures in the Front Range would trend in the midsixties with a chance of afternoon showers later in the week. The words were smudged and smeared, transposed on one another in irregular patterns. The air conditioner hummed behind me, and Mike yelled from upstairs, "HAVE YOU SEEN A BOX LABELED 'TOOLS'?" And even as I settled into this new place, I relived the stories of where I had come from. I unpacked the new and remembered the old, as though pedaling forward and backward can happen at the same time.

I tried to organize the kitchen as my mom would have done. I put the glasses in the cabinet that seemed most natural, but even that choice was an attempt to re-create the muscle memory I had learned at home. When I was growing up, the glasses were always left of the kitchen sink. So in Yuma, that's where they went too. I unpacked dishes that were given to us at our wedding. I unpacked spatulas and bath towels and the "As Seen on TV" popcorn machine that one friend had gifted to us with wideeyed enthusiasm. Each gift brought a name to mind, a ledger of people who had sourced the warm materials of home into our cool, sanitized house.

We needed the old, inherited things to settle here. We needed the Christmas ornaments our parents gave us, the stack of wedding cards we saved, the hope chest my dad built for me when I turned thirteen. We needed to fill empty closets with our favorite jackets, to fill the garage with a car racked with across-the-country miles. We needed to bring some remnants of home along with us as reminders that we weren't so alone, you know?

But as much as we loved and needed the old, we also needed the new, blank walls to fill with our own photos, cheap IKEA art, and misplaced nail holes. We needed an empty pantry to decide what sorts of foods would become our staples. More than that, we needed to feel a certain authority, to have a distinct awareness of ownership over the trajectory of our lives. And that begins with a sense of place. I suppose we wanted to exercise a measure of dominion, to stand taller in the knowledge that we were responsible for something and it mattered.

If we trace this impulse back to the beginning, we see that humanity began with God situating humans in a place. He put Adam in the Garden and also gave him a job to do—to tend and watch over it. So as much as we are children who want to be parented, we are also Kingdom builders who want to be released in authority. And after a lifetime of experiencing the former, there comes a point of insatiable desire for the latter. Usually this is around the time we move away from home.

A couple of weeks after moving into the Yuma house, we met our neighbors. David and Leta were nearly a decade ahead of us in both life and military, and they had three lovely, staggeringly respectful school-age children. We ran into the five of them while walking up our adjacent driveway and exchanged the normal courtesies. Leta sincerely apologized for not coming over sooner. David, the active-duty Marine, shook Mike's hand and asked him all sorts of questions about where he would work and, of course, where we came from.

"Colorado," Mike said, but perhaps the answer was already obvious from the Patagonia baseball cap on his head or the license plate fixed to the back of our car.

The Hugheses had recently moved to Yuma from Okinawa, Japan. We learned this first through their telling and later, more acutely, through the furniture in their living room. The room was identical to ours in dimension but staged so differently. Like us, they had pictures on the walls and a couch pushed beneath the main window, but against the back wall was an unusual entertainment center: six feet wide, with what looked like two wooden staircases pushed back to back, making a sort of modular pyramid that plateaued in the center for a television. The style was called step tansu, a form of cabinetry indigenous to Japan. They brought the entertainment center with them from their last duty station. Because we all fill the places we are with evidence of where we've been, don't we?

Home doesn't begin or end with a mailing address or a change in surname. I don't think it is ever a total reboot. It is more of an ellipsis than a period, a continuation rather than a conclusion. It tends to be an ongoing list of people and places and experiences that have mattered, that have changed us in one way or another. It is an echo of the good legacies we have witnessed.

In fact, home is a lot like a poorly categorized box containing all sorts of odds and ends: the surprising and familiar, the old and new, the bitter and sweet. It is mismatched in so many ways—not a start and end but an overlap, a tangle. We move away from it and bring it with us still.

But here is the good news: We never arrive to empty rooms empty handed.

# CHAPTER THREE

# WHEN I STOPPED RUNNING

## On Legacy and Identity

*It is a hard thing to leave any deeply routined life, even if you hate it.*

JOHN STEINBECK, *East of Eden*

My mom taught me how to run. As a child, I remember waking up to the slam of the screen door as she returned breathless and sweating from a morning jog. She smelled salty, with an edge of bitterness mixed into the day-old remnants of her perfume. At school, my friends would talk about their moms who sewed or worked as travel agents or sold makeup for Mary Kay, but my mom was the runner. I told this to people often, as if it were one of the more important details about me.

In the early 1990s, my mom didn't have sleek athletic outfits or new shoes or even a sports watch to accessorize her fitness. She ran in drawstring sweatpants, old gray

T-shirts, and a flat-billed Chicago Bulls baseball cap pulled low across the eyebrows. I don't think she had any idea that hip-hop stars dressed the exact same way. "I do it on purpose," she would say. "I dress like a boy so no one will bother me."

My mom ran with what she had—worn-out shoes and stolen time and two legs that found rhythm before sunrise. Running was a sanctuary for her, the place she went to be alone and to be quiet and to remember who she was apart from the noise.

On the infrequent occasions she ran in the evenings, my siblings and I would ride our bikes alongside her. My dad would occasionally come too, but a lot of times he would putter in the garage, rewrapping extension cords and reinstalling a single tennis ball that hung from the ceiling to ensure parking precision for our minivan. Most of the time my mom drove right through the tennis ball and nailed the deep freezer against the wall. "Whooooops," she would say, stretching the vowel to cover her guilt.

Perhaps this is why my dad spent so much time in the garage, trying to make those parking indicators more obvious. Really, he was trying to protect our deep freezer. The garage was to my dad what the sidewalk was to my mom: a place to organize things like tools and thoughts, a place that was quiet and personal, as all sanctuaries should be.

My mom would often leave the house exasperated

or exhausted or stressed to the brim, but after a run she would return miraculously revitalized. She would hum again. She would call me "sweetie" instead of my first name. It was a supernatural phenomenon, as if the miles staged an inner resurrection somewhere between the local high school and the long hill on Mirage Drive. Running equipped her with the resources I assumed all adults needed to manage their lives, specifically the boring tasks of holding a job and reading the newspaper.

I didn't understand it then, but I'm starting to understand it now: the deep desire of an overextended mom to have pockets of time to be invisible, to be unneeded, uninterrupted, and alone with a coherent thought for thirty whole minutes. Back then I thought she ran because she had an abundance of energy in middle age. Now I know that she was fostering an inner life long before the sun yawned a new day, protecting an essential piece of herself before her kids or her husband or her life could redirect her attention.

I became a runner because my mom was one, because I wanted to be like her and prove my devotion by investing in the things she loved first. Other girls wanted to get perms or wear makeup like their moms, but I wanted to run—not because the hobby was superior, but because a child notices the times her parents are living vibrant lives instead of muted ones, when they are operating as the most authentic versions of themselves.

By the time I grew up and moved to Yuma, running
was built into my identity. So it was on foot that I
learned my new home by its lettuce fields and irriga-
tion canals. Expensive parts of Yuma were landscaped
with exotic palm trees and red bougainvillea along crisp
white sidewalks. Ordinary parts were brown, dusty, and
neglected—cement on cement, stagnant desert creeping
toward rocky foothills, wide-open spaces summarized
in a single monotone. The sun consumed everything.
I ran with squinted eyes.

When something is built into your identity, it
becomes a home unto itself, an address where you go
to find a familiar version of yourself. Some people
thrive in the private space of a living room or the companionship around a dinner table. Others orient their
identity around where they dwell most comfortably
or most often: a job, a hobby, or a single achievement.
Most people, I think, characterize home strictly in the
domestic, geographic sense. But I found sacred communion in the steady breath of forward motion.

We see a hint of this in Scripture, too—a lot of bib-
lical interactions were active and physical. When the
Israelites were led out of Egypt, Miriam got all of the
women together, and they banged their tambourines as
they danced their way across the Red Sea.[4] King David
danced and sang with all his might before the Lord.[5]

After the power of God was revealed at Mount Carmel, Elijah tucked his cloak into his belt and he ran.[6] God, I think, is used to deciphering the movement of his people, discerning the contents of their hearts by the direction and frequency of their steps.

And for a restless, nomadic, cardio-loving soul like myself, it's especially intriguing that Jesus came to the physical location of Earth to build an invisible, transportable home within people. He shared the radical concept that the epicenter of spiritual life was not contained in the walls of a synagogue or religious institution or even at a set address, but in the souls of human beings. The most sacred part of us is also the most mobile. The life of the soul can easily relocate across the miles of the desert or nations on the globe or even the longer distance between heaven and earth. Faith is a bridge between places— a point of continuity in a transient life. And especially in the military, where a person collects addresses in bulk, I like to think the roots of the soul can redeem a shortage of the more geographic kind.

Perhaps this is why running was where my prayers found expression, with words or without. It was where I processed my day, where I wrung out my mad and sad and lonely. Running taught me that faith could be fostered on the move, that I could be spiritually grounded while physically active. In time, I considered running to be the unchangeable flavor of my Christianity, the part that Jesus was naturally most impressed with. I fully expected I would be eighty-seven years old and still lacing up white sneakers with quivering fingers, still beginning the day on the run with a bobbing white ponytail and tanned, wrinkly arms swinging to and fro.

Away from family and familiarity, dislodged from everything I had previously known, I attached myself to this one association: I was a runner. It was part heritage from my mom, part spiritual practice, and part delusion that if I were only thin and fast enough, then everything would be all right. But just as we can be displaced from geographic homes, so too we can be forced to move from the addresses upon which we've built our whole identity. We can move on from all sorts of places, visible and not.

And in the second year of Yuma, I injured my right hip. Badly. To be specific, I tore through the lining. "Too much running," the doctor said as he scheduled my surgery. "Can you find an alternative activity?" He said this hopefully, as if he were the first skinny person to ever suggest I try Pilates.

Suddenly, after being a runner who wakes up early and completes marathons and has a functional relationship with Gatorade, I became a broken-down athlete, the sort who wears old race T-shirts while walking on crutches, the sort who grocery shops with an electric wheelchair alongside the elderly, the sort who is really angry and disappointed and doesn't know how to process her emotions while sitting still, while distinctly *not* sweating.

This injury crept in cunningly like a betrayal. It displaced me from the home I never considered vulnerable. I had been a foreigner to many places but never to my own body. Who was I if I wasn't a runner? I mean, did Jesus even like me without muscle tone? I could deal with the temporal nature of a mailing address, but this ending seemed more personal. It took away a part of my identity that I had considered fixed and sure, the part I had leaned into to cope with all the other changes in my life.

A few years earlier my mom had stopped running too. In a common and familiar runner's tale, she ruined both knees from "pounding the pavement." This is her favorite running phrase, the one she will most often use if you ask her about her running. In the discussion, she will describe the violence of her former foot strike by loudly slapping her palms together each time she says the word *pounding*. This makes her a runner all the more, I think. She can't describe a single one of her life's passions without animating her body.

I was the one to pick her up from the hospital the day of her first knee surgery. And as I wheeled her out in a wheelchair, I remember sensing this profound disappointment in her, like she wasn't just recovering from a physical injury but ushering in the end of an era.

There would be no more running for her. Doctors

said she could ride the bike or elliptical machine at the
gym, but at the time these were the sorts of activities we
relegated to pretty girls who went to the gym to meet the
muscle-y boys who wore cutoff tank tops. Later, when she
was healthy again, my mom would demolish this assumption when she'd hop on an elliptical, turn the resistance
up to a million, and make it her slave for sixty continuous
minutes.

But at the beginning, or should I say the end, there
was only the simple sense of loss.

The same sense ate at me those years later. I flew
home to Colorado to have my hip surgery and recover
at my mom's house. It seemed appropriate since she
knew what this kind of loss felt like. The surgery itself
was short. But the recovery was long and sort of humil-
iating.

For instance, my first physical therapy assignment
after surgery was to lie facedown on the ground. That's
it. That was the whole exercise, to lie on the ground like
a log, like a seal, like I was dead. The physical therapist
told me to put a timer on for ten minutes and breathe
through the pain as my hip and abdominal muscles
remembered how to stretch. Apparently when a part of
the body is injured, the adjoining muscles and tendons
constrict around it to protect it. So the act of lying pros-
trate on the carpet was a command to my body: *Let go!*
My mom would do this exercise with me, her shoulder
rubbing mine, our heads turned to the same side so she

couldn't see my sideways tears pooling in my ear and wetting the edges of her carpet.

Within a week or so, I practiced sitting up. Mike came and stayed for that first week, propping me up on the toilet seat, helping me stand up when I was done. It was like being ninety-five years old all of a sudden, as frail as I was constipated, wishing my mom had installed handrails along her bathroom walls and not wasted her money on the generic brand of Metamucil. I kept apologizing to Mike, to my mom, for being so needy. It was weird to need someone else so fundamentally, to receive without being able to offer anything in return.

A week or so later I was able to get around on crutches. This was a huge victory. I had my mom take a picture of me crutching around the house while I wore sunglasses indoors like a celebrity. Even then, however, my primary activity was lying in bed, bending my legs, knees to chest, one at a time. The surgeon had prescribed a rotation machine that I strapped my right leg into from thigh to foot. It was a sort of luge that rolled up and down, pushing my leg from straight to bent over and over again. The machine made a squeaky, groaning sound, similar to when an old door is opening or a feral cat is dying. For eight hours a day I was prescribed to use this thing, which meant that my full-time job was being adjoined to a robot leg that serenaded my recovery with the sounds of a horror film.

The tragedy, of course, was not that I was a twenty-four-year-old woman recovering from major hip surgery. It was that Instagram was not yet around to keep me company.

It is so difficult to let go of something that feels as essential as a foundation, whether you lose it by accident or against your will or through choices you never intended to make. If it's not running, it could be a job that you loved or a relationship that had become a part of you. It could be a divorce, or a dream you chased that didn't pan out like you thought it would. Important appendages to our lives get amputated sometimes, and although you'd like to dust yourself off and get on with it, there is a profound sense of loss that you have to sort through first. And you are allowed to be devastated for a time, even if no one else understands how much that thing, that version of home, mattered to you.

Before you get to the part where you can see the silver lining, before you believe with hope and conviction in God's redemptive plan, and before you are able to take a deep breath and realize it's all going to be okay, there is the stretch where you are just disappointed, plain and simple; where there is a sense of panic over what was demolished; where you feel puzzled by your own life, cosmically let down; where you don't really want to talk about it or think about it or be productive in any way and all you want to do is watch back to back marathons of home improvement shows and consider ways to make Joanna Gaines your new best friend. This, you think, will make you feel better.

Faith will rise in a moment, but for right now, you just need to mourn.

Maybe this is all a key part of growing up—not just leaving home geographically, but learning to leave behind the parts of your identity that you thought were enduring, the ways you felt most at home within yourself. It seems to me that maturity grows, not exclusively but heartily, on the fringes of profound disappointment. You and I confront so many surprise endings in a single lifetime, and perhaps this is how we discover exactly what is disposable and what is essential. It's how we realize how resilient we are.

I wonder, too, if God doesn't use this sort of transience to draw us to himself, if he doesn't occasionally wring out the things we don't want to give him, in order to expose all the ways we don't trust him. Out come insecurity, fear, and doubt, the lies we've believed about ourselves and about him. Out comes the mindless religion—the empty habits and vague affections. All the feeble hooks we've hung our worth on, every striving part of us tumbles out until we are emptied of our own merit, of all pretenses, laid bare exactly as we are, perhaps facedown in the literal sense, with crutches and an enormous ice pack standing by. It's here, stripped down to the beams, that we figure out who we are and what we truly believe. We get to the authentic relationship, to the honest posture of the heart, to faith that's birthed from a willingness to love God not from a place of control but from a place of surrender.

Ephesians 1:11-12 (MSG) says, "It's in Christ that we find out who we are and what we are living for. Long before we first heard of Christ and got our hopes up, he had his eye on us, had designs on us for glorious living, part of the overall purpose he is working out in everything and everyone." I'm quick to forget this, but the truth is that intimacy with God is secured by the reliability of his grace, not by the quality of our performance. And it's because of this propensity to forget that we must be reminded often and acutely of just how deep and wide that grace is, how central the Cross is to reconciling us to our fundamental identity.

My friend Tammy talks about this a lot—about how crucial it is to understand identity through the lens of who we are in Christ. "No one can take from you what they did not give," she says. And I think what she means is that when you hitch your stability to the sturdiness of Christ, specifically to who and what he says you are— beloved, adopted, forgiven, and chosen—you become sturdy too. In fact, you become more than resilient. You become untouchable. Because no city or person or circumstance, no single loss, can take away from you what it did not give: your value or identity. Only the Creator can tell the created what it was made for.

So when I don't know where else to begin, when I'm lying on the floor asking the big "Who am I?" questions all over again, I think of what Tammy says. And I go back to the beginning, to the only sturdy place, to the declared assurance that I was loved before I did anything at all, that I was chosen before I had the opportunity to audition, that before God laid down the earth's foundations, "he had [me] in mind, had settled on [me] as the focus of his love, to be made whole and holy by his love."[7]

This process of being "made whole and holy by his love" is often uncomfortable, though it's always productive. It is a form of rehabilitation by way of wringing out, breaking down, letting go. Then again, my faith tends to grow the fastest when I get to the end of myself, when I feel that I have nothing to offer. But it's here that I learn for myself that God redeems every broken place, that his goodness is not contingent on my own. There's nothing left to prove, no ladder left to climb. Ironically, it's when we stop running that we discover it was God's grace chasing us all along.

In the initial months after surgery, every time I'd see a runner making her way along the sidewalk, I would feel a sharp twinge of loss. From the window of my car, I'd watch another person run and remember the rhythm of steps and burn of breath, the sideways sashay of my ponytail, the heat emanating through the bottoms of my shoes. And I would get terribly homesick for that feeling.

Eventually, though, the sense of loss faded. Over time it hurt less and less to see other people running, the same way it takes time before you're ready to see an old boyfriend date other people. The initial reaction of sadness and envy slowly transitioned to a vague sentimentality, then to a positive memory, until finally it didn't sting at all. My process of letting go was marked by passing runners, one by one, by how easy it was to spectate as they experienced a liberty I had left behind.

Soon, I sensed a different sort of productivity swelling in me, one thing giving way to another. I knew I was becoming whole in an unexpected way. I could feel myself changing—feel my will being reshaped as through the ebb and flow of a new tide. And that's the thing about a tide. Sometimes it carries you into a place you never intended to go. Oswald Chambers writes, "We are uncertain of the next step, but we are certain of God. As soon as we abandon ourselves to God and do the task He has placed closest to us, He begins to fill our lives with surprises."[8] And this is what happened to me, it seems.

Because when I stopped running, I started to write. And when I did, I found that buried in every story was a testimony I didn't expect. All my life has been a slow discovery of the sturdiness of God against the fleeting nature of everything else.

Even the pathways I've used to connect to God, the praise habits I've cultivated, have come in seasons and in spurts. For a time it was running; for now it is writing. For you, it may look different. Interacting with God may be taking a walk or singing songs in the shower or exploring the outdoors or studying the Word down to its Hebrew or Greek origins. Your most comfortable spiritual practice might be silence or song, intellect or wonder, discussion or private contemplation. Whatever the natural outlet is, it is a tool, a gift, but often a temporary one. You could be a singer who loses her voice for a time, a hiker who moves away from the mountains, an exquisite friend who is suddenly forced to build new relationships. Or say, for example, you're used to having long devotional times in the morning, covering chapters of Scripture and meditating on their meaning while slowly sipping coffee—but then you become a parent, and morning meditation is condensed to the space between the washer and the dryer. Worship becomes the prayers you whisper in the middle of the night when you're so tired but your wee ones are crying out your name. God is accessible still, but you have to find a new method to respond to him. You must learn how to be resourceful with the time and skill and capacity you have at the moment, even if it's not what it was before. This, I think, is a severe but beautiful grace.

Because the spiritual practice itself is not what connects us to God. The Cross is what connects us to God.

So now I wonder if the loss of something we consider essential is a way to learn that we don't have to be productive for God in order to be known by him. We don't have to be good at something to be loved by him. Our spiritual home is not found in an activity or skill set. It's found in a person, in God himself. And each talent or ability is a pathway rather than a destination, a means of letting go.

It's all an invitation to come home to him.

# CHAPTER FOUR

# STEADFAST

## *On Marriage*

*I don't mean what other people mean when they speak of
a home, because I don't regard a home as a . . . well, as
a place, a building . . . a house . . . of wood, bricks, stone.
I think of a home as being a thing that two people have
between them in which each can . . . well, nest.*

TENNESSEE WILLIAMS, *The Night of the Iguana*

Our wedding was in January 2009, shortly after Beyoncé
released the song "Single Ladies," which felt like a personal
gift not just to humanity but specifically to my wedding
reception. The groomsmen wore their sunglasses indoors
for the evening reception in addition to, regrettably, the
bulk of our formal wedding photos. They also popped
their collars and requested Kanye West songs from the
DJ while the more seasoned adults requested hits by Neil
Diamond. In both cases, the DJ was asked to play "something we can actually dance to."

In more important current events, Barack Obama
had just become president, and less than a month after

taking office he ordered an additional seventeen thousand troops deployed to Afghanistan. The U.S. had been
at war for eight years by the time Mike finished his training, and we moved to Yuma that summer. And when we
got there, many of the families we met had gone through
two, three, and sometimes four or more deployments,
each between six and twelve months. They had tallied
personal sacrifice in years of detachment and family sep-
aration, so they wore deployments like badges of honor,
like chevrons of legitimacy, considering each a terrible
yet often mandatory tryout to becoming an insider in
the military community. By the time Mike and I arrived,
it felt like we were already behind.

To be honest, I didn't even realize how personal
war could be until we moved to Yuma and lived in a
neighborhood where at any given time several houses
were decorated in American flags and an enormous banner hung across the garage that read "Welcome Home
Daddy!" I'm embarrassed to admit that now—how
naive I was. But I learned quickly. And once you see the
cost, you want to do your part to bear the burden, just
as when you go over to someone else's house for dinner,
the first thing you ask is if there's anything you can help
with in the kitchen. Often the host says no, but it's
important that you volunteer. It's important that you
try. It says something about your character to be eager
to contribute.

Shortly after Mike and I got married, Mike's mom

brought to our attention an obscure verse in the Old
Testament: Deuteronomy 24:5. It says, "If a man has
recently married, he must not be sent to war or have
any other duty laid on him. For one year he is to be free
to stay at home and bring happiness to the wife he has
married" (NIV). Mike's mom committed to pray this over
Mike and me.

Of course I wanted a year with Mike, and I believe he
wanted it too, but he was also a Marine who was eager
to help in the kitchen, so to speak. He wanted to experience the war of his generation, to be a helpful volunteer.
In the meantime, he was happy to go on date nights with
me and pick up milk on the way home from work. But
quietly, not even secretly, he was desperate to deploy.
At every opportunity, he raised his hand. It's a habit he
maintains to this day. And we both understand why: This
is what he was trained to do—to serve his country in the
midst of conflict. And until he deployed, everything else
seemed like rehearsal, like busywork, like being an under-
study for a role that everyone else was already playing.

We got our first year together, which might be another
way of saying that Mike's mom is very good at praying.
I know a lot of people talk about their first year of marriage as very challenging, but for us it really wasn't. For
us, it was a year of consistent, seemingly mundane discoveries that each felt like a revelation.

For example, I learned that I was not, in fact, as
clean as I originally supposed. Because unlike my
spouse, I firmly believed in the necessity of a junk
drawer. Where else would a person keep the pens that
don't work and batteries that may or may not be used?
Additionally, I learned with astonishment that there's
such a thing as preventative maintenance on a car,
that some people don't just drive their cars until they
break down and then weep openly on the side of the
road. Some people actually keep track of things like
oil changes and pay stubs and the exact year they're
due for a tetanus shot.

The learning curve of our first year of marriage was
modest, I think, because every other part of our lives so
easily overlapped. Mike and I processed our new careers
at the same time, growing in knowledge and responsibility. Connection was easy for us then. We had no kids
yet, no big hindrances to spending enormous amounts
of time together. So that's what we did. If marriage is
a matter of concentric circles, during that first year we
nearly eclipsed each other with how much we shared.
And I suppose that's what made it seem sort of easy,
as if two becoming one were the most natural thing
in the world.

Five months after my own wedding, I flew back to
Colorado to be a bridesmaid in my friend Arica's wedding. In the bridal suite I reported back to my friends
that marriage was great and simple. I dispensed empty

platitudes such as "As long as you both love Jesus, it all works out!" and "Communication really is key!" It's not that this advice is wrong, necessarily. It's just that it hadn't been personally tested in my life yet.

Some people say that marriage is really hard. Others say it's really easy. I think you don't know what marriage is until you've lived through both gears, the easy and the hard.

And for us the hard eventually came. After the first year, on the very week of our first anniversary, Mike was selected to support a training exercise in Camp Pendleton, a base about three and a half hours away from Yuma. He moved there for five months, and in the same week he returned home, the phone rang again. This time he was put on a small team being deployed to Afghanistan. It was called a transition team, a small group of Marines that would embed with the Afghans and live among them outside the walls of an American base—or in military terms, "outside the wire"—teaching and equipping them to be a self-sufficient military in their own right.

Mike was thrilled, obviously.

I was hysterical.

In the first year, we had a full twelve months together. Over the course of the next fifteen months, Mike and I lived together for a total of two weeks.

But here's the mercy in it all: We got exactly what was prayed for.

When Mike would call home from Afghanistan, it was always from an unknown number. The home screen of my cell phone would flash a series of zeros and ones, and I would fumble my hands to unlock his voice. Each time he led with "Hey, baby." Three syllables spoken so warmly and evenly that they almost rhymed.

Sometimes the connection would be crystal clear. But more often it was very bad, a heavily delayed discussion shouted down two ends of an echoing tunnel. Mike was deployed to a patrol base with unreliable power and limited Internet, so the phone and e-mails were our only options—no FaceTime or Skype. When he would call home once a week or so, our conversation would spontaneously drop at least twice. At the beginning of the deployment I supposed that this was because a bomb went off or combatants infiltrated the base. But it was never that dire. Deployment is cartoonishly frightening in the beginning simply because it's so foreign. Your imagination goes wild in the pockets of what you don't know. Soon, though, I learned that calls dropped not by exception, but as a general rule. Interruptions were ordinary: midsentence, midbreath, right at the good part of the story.

For months I carried my phone in my hand as if it were an extension of my body. I answered it in public bathrooms and on restaurant loading docks, carried it with me on runs and set it faceup on the table at dinner with friends. Sometimes I would check it halfway through a shower, wiping soap out of my eyes and shaking water from my fingertips, just to make sure it was on and I hadn't missed a phone call. We e-mailed fairly regularly, too, but there was something about his voice, the warmth and tone and timbre, that made communication more personal, that proved I was connected to him in real time. Especially in the beginning, answering the phone seemed like an act of fidelity, as though being available for every call were the single sacrament of our marriage, as if I were honoring him by not moving on with life in his absence.

I remember the first time I missed one of Mike's phone calls. When I saw the notification on the cell phone screen, my heart sank and tears sprang to my eyes. I felt guilty, like a failure. "What if he doesn't call again?" I asked myself.

But then he would call again. Eventually he called enough times in weekly succession that it formed an expectation that he was just fine and would continue to be. The habit created the illusion of safety and control. So over time the cloud of impending doom felt less oppressive, as if through the routine of carrying on I convinced myself that I actually could. The indicator of this shift is when you're able to miss a phone call without feeling like it's the end of the world. Or maybe it's when you answer the phone but are distracted still, more in tune with the life in front of you than with the one on the phone. The new normal, I found, was in being disconnected from one another, but no longer bothered by it.

On the other end of the phone was a husband who was also distracted, but in a different way. Mike always sounded so very far away, not just because he was physically, but because he was mentally and emotionally, too. The Marine never spoke harshly on the phone, was never brusque or aggressive, but I could occasionally catch a faint trace of those characteristics in his voice, the residue of a persona he embodied only in uniform and at war. I found traces of his deployment life in his deployment voice, a man caught between the roles of warrior and husband, inadvertently bringing the lingering scent of one into the other.

In the beginning, I expected Mike to remain completely engaged as a husband and friend. I wanted him to corroborate my life as he had always done, to bear witness to every detail—even if only in my retelling. I wanted to talk as if we had time to spare, to discuss my job and my workouts and my recent discovery of *Veronica Mars* on Netflix. Most of all, I wanted to navigate the razor-sharp emotionality of deployment with the only person I assumed could understand.

But Mike was preoccupied, which meant he wasn't returning my love in the particular ways I wanted him to. His emotional capacity was redirected for a time. As it turns out, a man engages with his wife quite differ-

ently and with a little more reserve when he's living outside the wire in a combat zone than when he's sitting on
the couch, having a bowl of ice cream. It was as if he had
to dim the lights on the domestic side of his brain for a
little while, to go into energy-save mode when it came to
keeping up with how I felt about my most recent haircut or when the dog last had her nails clipped. And this
came as a surprise to me, because Mike is so stubbornly
meticulous, so thorough and engaged, especially in our
relationship. Reluctantly, though, I learned that a warrior must occasionally detach from his allies to become
more vigilant toward his enemies. He must become
strategically impenetrable to friends, to family, even to a
wife with the access key of a wedding band, so that all of
his attention can be spent, you know, living dangerously
and staying alive.

I suppose this phenomenon occurs everywhere, in all
of us, including those outside the military. It happens
when an executive works long hours or a student retreats
to private corners of a library, when a writer writes in
solitude or an athlete trains in the privacy of his own
ambition. In order to create, to defend, to innovate, each
of us must occasionally retreat to a singular place that is
only ours. Sometimes important work requires a door
that locks behind us. And this is tricky if all your stability
is rooted in one human person. Because if home is where
the heart is, what happens when your heart is distracted,
deployed, or detached?

Each of us lived a little more privately from the other in that year, mystified by where we overlapped. Mike couldn't or wouldn't say much about what he was doing. And by comparison, anything I had to say felt silly or small. E-mails and phone calls became more about checking in than actual connection, as if we were playing a game of Marco Polo, routinely volleying the same pointless questions back and forth—"How was your day?" "How are you doing?" "Did you sleep last night?"—hoping the sound of our echoing voices would somehow bring us closer together even though the answers remained the same.

Fine. Okay.

Talk soon.

Love you.

Bye.

Mike was distracted, yes, by the whole business of deployment. But I was distracted too, by the business of trying to find a new, endurable normal without him. So the phone calls became shorter and further between. It was a matter of busyness, sure, but the real reason was that after a while each conversation felt like a small failure in connection, like we didn't really know how to talk to each other anymore—how to dig beneath the surface and land at the matters of the heart.

Of course, physical distance isn't a requirement for relational distance. One or both of you can be in the same place, the same house, even in the same room and be consumed by something else—say, the task of parenting or working from home or taking a class online. You can sit right next to each other and be absorbed by your phone, reading the news or scrolling through social media or texting with friends. Sure, you're together, but he's following a sport you don't care about while you're giggling at an inside joke you're cultivating with someone else. Time together can mean sitting in front of a television or doing chores alongside each other—being productive simultaneously without ever being present. At least for me, one of the great surprises of marriage is that it is so easy to become estranged from someone you love, even when they are within arm's reach. It's as if we drift by default.

My first encounter with this accidental drifting was during the deployment. Suddenly we were distant from each other in more than geography, and we didn't know what to do about it except to call home, to answer the phone, to keep showing up for each other in the ways we could through a season that was barren of easy or frequent conversation.

And if I'm honest with you, during this time I felt helpless and lonely and emotionally abandoned. I wondered if this temporary estrangement would cling to us like a disease; if it would become permanent, chronic, terminal; if it would ruin everything. Our grip on each other was slipping, and I wasn't at all sure that things would ever be the same. I worried that if a combat deployment didn't cost the life of my husband, it might very well cost the life of my marriage. And my most desperate prayer to God was that he would somehow preserve our unity, that he would step in as the stability between us. Because if home is where the heart is, our hearts had to be entrusted to a better, more permanent place than each other.

In our wedding ceremony, Mike and I took Communion. My hands shook as I held the piece of bread and sipped from the brass cup of wine. To be honest, my deepest thoughts of the moment were not of religious piety but of concern that I would pour the entire cup of red liquid down the front of my wedding dress. For this reason, I thought—for the first time ever—that perhaps Communion should be served with a long plastic straw. Mike slipped his arm around my lower back, steadying me, and together we bowed our heads to pray in remembrance and recognition of Jesus' sacrifice.

It matters to me—especially now—that the very first thing we did after saying our vows was redirect our attention to a better, more beautiful banner of love. I like to think that this act of Communion was the first step of an early habit, that the place our marriage began is the same place it will return to over and over again, as an altar, a lighthouse, a home of record: there, holding the bread and the wine, whispering the only words we could muster—"Thank you. Thank you. Thank you"—as we took in the magnitude of the sacrificial love of God with quivering lips and clammy palms and the sound of a piano playing in the background.

I like to think that if we return to this place over and over again, if we stop enough times and bear witness to how Jesus loved us, it will become the central point of stability in our lives. And maybe then the nature of our commitment will be shaped by what we have witnessed with regularity: forgiveness and restoration, wholeness on the other side of brokenness, the daring hope that nothing is beyond the redemptive power of the Cross.

I love how Timothy Keller frames this kind of commitment:

> In any relationship, there will be frightening spells in which your feelings of love seem to dry up. And when that happens you must remember that the essence of a marriage is that it is a covenant, a commitment, a promise of future love. So what do you do? You do the acts of love, despite your lack of feeling. You may not feel tender, sympathetic, and eager to please, but in your actions you must *be* tender, understanding, forgiving, and helpful. And, if you do that, as time goes on you will not only get through the dry spells, but they will become less frequent

and deep, and you will become more constant
in your feelings. This is what can happen if you
decide to love.[9]

I've found that it's easy to make marriage a sequence
of reactions, to summarize it based on how strong the
compulsion is to "be tender, sympathetic, and eager to
please." In fact, I've found my default setting is to be
more a consumer of love than a dispenser of it, to set
my husband as the standard for good behavior and echo
his best attempts. *If you are nice to me, I'll be nice to you.
Honor me. I'll honor you.*
*But you first.*
*You first.*
*You first.*
Yet there is a better standard of steadfast love: Jesus,
the one who promises, "I will go first." And he did.
Though we were sinful, Christ absorbed punishment
on our behalf. Though we failed, he forgave. This is the
ultimate standard of faithfulness: the absolute, uncondi-
tional love of God.

One of the mercies, then, of long-distance relationship or any hard season of marriage might be the way
it drains the consumerism out of us, how it draws out
the contingencies and impurities we accidentally let slip
between vows of "for better or for worse." It teaches us
about the decision to love in the absence of feeling like
it. Here, in gaps of geography and connection, we learn

the grit of loving and serving even when we can't see the return on investment yet.

As for Mike and me, when we didn't know where else to begin, we defaulted to tiny steps of faithfulness. Mike called home even when the conversations were uninspired, and I kept answering the phone. I sent him expensive care packages of beef jerky that he promptly gave away to other guys who liked it more. He ordered me four-inch platform heels when I mentioned offhand that I could use a pair of "reasonable black work shoes."

And in between the cracks of our insufficient tries were prayers that banked on the hope that God, in his own mysterious sufficiency, could hold us together far better than we knew how to do ourselves.

# CHAPTER FIVE

# THE FRONT DOOR

*On Fear*

*Peace—that was the other name for home.*

KATHLEEN NORRIS, *Woman's Home Companion*

When I was a kid, I was afraid of being home alone. Every creak or pop in the house, every time the heater buzzed or the wind rattled through an old window, I took it as a sign that a criminal was probably in the house looking for me. Like the rest of the millennial generation, I was coached from birth on how extraordinarily special I was. I understood that my dreams were very important, that I was smart and kind and good at basically everything. So naturally I considered myself an irresistible candidate for kidnapping.

When I was growing up, we lived in a very safe neighborhood in Colorado Springs, where everyone waved hello to each other and drove either a minivan or a Subaru Outback with a Focus on the Family bumper sticker on the back. Hatchbacks were everywhere, and JNCO jeans were considered the most violent affront to the pleasantness of our community. Truly, there was nothing to be afraid of.

Yet on the few afternoons I was home alone, I devoted my time to frantically plotting a catastrophe strategy. I decided that if I were confronted with a robber, I did not want to hide. It seemed to me that if I burrowed beneath blankets or wedged myself underneath the bed and was discovered, I would be trapped. So in choosing between fight or flight on the spectrum of overreaction, I decided that flight was my best option.

During those afternoons, I camped out next to the front door. I didn't even sit down. I just stood ready and alert like a self-appointed sentry, looking out the window and counting the minutes until my parents got home.

Even now as an adult, when I linger near my own front door, I remember the afternoons I waited for my parents to come home. It's funny how certain places act as bookmarks of emotion, how a song is related to a memory or a smell takes you back to a specific moment in time. The door, to me, stood as a passageway to my history with fear. And it's the sort of history that escorts me right up to the present.

During the year that Mike was deployed, I was once startled awake from dead sleep in the middle of the night by an urgent banging on my front door. Not just staccato rapping—loud, echoing, impolite banging, like the thunderous beat of a kick drum. Someone with an enormous fist was bruising the center of my front door, and I thought the door might collapse or fold under the weight of the noise. The dog barked frantically, and I jumped out of bed, disoriented and afraid. My hands were shaking. Really, my whole body was shaking.

In that house, the front door had a rectangular window across the top of it, and from the top of the stairs one could peer through the glass pane and see who was knocking. That night I ran from my bedroom to the top of the stairs and caught a glimpse through the window of a Marine in uniform. He looked haunted. The bill of his hat trapped the light of an angled flashlight and sent it back toward his face, his skin a ghostly terrain of shadows.[10]

The time was 4:18 a.m., and I was alone.

"PMO! PMO! This is PMO! Open the door!" the Marine shouted.[11]

The police were at my door in the middle of the night. Fear rippled beneath my skin like an electrical current. The dog raced down the stairs and clawed at the door, barking manically. I followed her, grabbed her by the collar, and cracked the door open as she pedaled her front paws in the air. I didn't even have time to get a word out before the officer said, "Ma'am. I need you to gather everyone in your household and meet me on the driveway immediately. All of your children, your pets, your spouse. Everyone. You need to do this as quickly as you can. Do you understand me?"

I nodded and swallowed hard. My heart was beating wildly, thumping in sync with the speed of sprinting steps I imagined using to run away.

The Marine turned quickly on his heel before I had time to ask a question. As I closed the door, I heard the percussive sound of pounding on my neighbors' doors. Thick fists on heavy doors like a drum line parading down the street. What was happening?

I closed the door and put on shoes and glasses. In under a minute, I met the officer on my driveway, leashed dog in hand.

"Is this everyone in your household?" he said urgently.

"Yes. Just me and my dog," I replied.

"This is everyone? There are no children with you in the house?"

"No. Just me. My husband is deployed, and we don't have any kids."

He repeated the question twice more, confused and disbelieving that a military spouse could live alone, particularly in her healthy childbearing years. On a clipboard he filled out a form with quick, urgent flicks of the hand. He didn't explain the situation, didn't offer a reason for why I was standing in my driveway in my pajamas, talking to a police officer at four in the morning.

Without looking me in the eye, he ordered me to cross the street and stand with other families who were now congregating. Children in footie pajamas held blankets and teddy bears; men and women standing side by side wore athletic jackets over sleeping clothes. As I approached with my dog, I overheard the conversation between evacuated neighbors.

"... there is a shooter ... a gunman ... threatening suicide ... on the patio ... they're worried about stray bullets into the back of the houses ..."

Then we heard a single gunshot muffled and far away. Everyone held their breath, wondering what it meant, until one of the neighbors—a man who didn't exactly look like a Marine under his early morning stubble—said, "Well." Then he sighed. "That means it's over."

And he was right.

Ten minutes later another officer came and casually said, "You all can go home now." The crowd silently dispersed, but I don't think anyone went back to sleep.

Details of the incident trickled out throughout the next day. Whispers of a domestic dispute infused with too much alcohol. The Marine had just returned from deployment, and everyone wondered if the notorious culprit of PTSD was to blame. He had wandered onto his back patio with a loaded gun. The police responded. Death arrived by his own hand.

After that night, even more so than before, I eyed the front door fearfully, especially after dark. When I peered through the door window from the top of the stairs, I half expected someone to be there, someone I didn't know. It made me feel like a child again, sensitive to noises and sounds, creating bad omens from unmoving shadows, constantly brainstorming my reaction to imagined scenarios. I spent so much time scared, which was bothersome because it seemed that if fear had remained true to size, I should have outgrown it by now. Since I was an adult, it seemed like I should feel more powerful, more in control, especially when staying home alone.

The front door was particularly scary during the months of deployment, not just because of those childhood memories or the incident of the evacuation, but because the front door is where casualty notification officers arrive when a service member has been killed. So during deployment, when you're feeling vulnerable and scared and lonely, the most suspicious intrusion in your world isn't a call from an unknown phone number or a seedy-looking stranger who stops you on the street. It's an unexpected knock on the door from trustworthy men in uniform. It's a surprise that finds you at home.

And so it wasn't just at nighttime that I felt a little

squirrely around the door. It was when I heard whispers
of casualties in the region Mike was patrolling, or when I
heard nothing at all from him for days or weeks on end.
Silence was the worst form of suspense. I worried about
the front door when I was bored or when I was lonely,
and most of all when I received an e-mail from Mike
that was so charming and gushy that I thought, *Oh my
gosh I love him so much I might die*, which was quickly
followed by the accompanying thought: *OH MY GOSH
WHAT IF HE DIES?*

Ironically, it was when I felt the strongest pangs of
love that I simultaneously felt the strongest pangs of fear.
And that's when I began going a little bit crazy, tinting
all warm feelings with imagined doom. In the absence
of an accurate understanding of where Mike was in
Afghanistan or what he was doing, I imagined my own
reality for him, and it was far, far worse.

When I couldn't sleep at night, I conjured up worst-
case scenarios of wartime combat and death and graphic
injury and escorted them across my consciousness, one
by one. I pulverized my emotions with horrific scenarios
as if I believed the trauma would create a callus, and that
callus would protect me from pain if my fears were ever
realized.

Sometimes I even poked around the imagined scene of
a casualty notification, auditing the details. What would I
do if it happened to me? Would my knees buckle? Would
I cry immediately or be stunned, standing there wide-eyed

and motionless? Who would I call first? My mom? My sister? Mike's family? What would I say? Would I be wearing makeup? Maybe just getting home from work, heels still on? Dressed in business casual?

When would it happen? What would it look like? How would I feel? Is it possible to rehearse or prepare for such a moment?

I think when we're afraid, we tend to grasp at any measure of control, even if it's purely imagined. So that's what I did while Mike was deployed. I grasped at mental preparedness that did nothing to combat the fear. It did the opposite. It fed the monster. Brené Brown calls this "foreboding joy," combating feelings of joy with imagined tragedy.[12] She says this is a sort of armor we use to protect ourselves from the risk of fully living. She does not recommend it.

A couple of weeks after that evacuation, I was in a crowded living room with friends for Thanksgiving. The meal was hosted by a family I didn't know very well, but I had tagged along with dear couple friends of ours, Caleb and Justine, who had adopted me into their holiday plans on a day I was enormously homesick.

The living room was full of folding tables with plastic tablecloths, seated families celebrating far from home, spouses caught in the center of deployment, and pilots who hollered call signs across the table when asking for more mashed potatoes. Kids ran around barefoot and screaming. Truly, it was lovely, but also only partially satisfying. On holidays I think everyone wants to be around familiar people, specifically around family, and so that meal felt like a pretend Thanksgiving, like I was just accidentally overeating on a Thursday afternoon.

Justine, Caleb, and I left the house at the same time. They walked to their car hand in hand, so happily married and geographically colocated that I surely would have internally annihilated them with envy if they weren't such incredibly generous, likable people. Head down, I walked to my car, looking at my cell phone for the millionth time that day to see if Mike had called. He hadn't. I hadn't heard from him in days. Then I drove away.

I didn't know it then, but once we said good-bye and buckled ourselves into our respective vehicles, Caleb checked his phone and realized he had missed several calls. From the passenger seat, Justine watched his cheerful demeanor change.

Caleb was the casualty notification officer for the unit—the same unit that Mike was in. And while we were eating and laughing and celebrating Thanksgiving, there had been a casualty. There was no word yet if it had occurred domestically or internationally, but Caleb was being urgently summoned to notify the family.

As I was driving home, I had no idea that Caleb was preparing for a notification. I didn't know that the casualty was from the same job code as Mike's or that the Marine was on an individual assignment just as Mike was. I didn't know that, in the absence of better information, the assumption was that the casualty was in fact Mike and that Caleb was mentally preparing to notify his friend's wife that her husband was dead.

More than that, I didn't know that as Caleb prepared for notification, Justine pulled into my neighborhood, slow and quiet in her tiny Nissan. For hours on Thanksgiving night she waited near my house, just a few streets away, standing watch just in case an unfamiliar vehicle with two Marines and a chaplain pulled up and somberly knocked on my front door. Later, she told me that if I had to bear that news, she didn't want me to do it alone. In a discreet act of love, she guarded my front door the whole time I wasn't looking.

I did not have to bear the news that night.

Mike was alive and far removed from the circumstance that was being relayed to the notification officials. But after I heard about the series of these events, Mike's life felt like a sharp mercy, and the memory of that day pierces me with sadness still, since someone else did have to bear the news, since this sort of thing happens so terribly often, and since I don't understand why—why it wasn't me, why it wasn't Mike, when it so easily could have been.

But now when I revisit that memory, I think less of

the danger of the moment, less of the lingering questions, and more of the watchfulness of my friend Justine. I imagine her in her car, sitting and waiting, praying for Mike and for me. I imagine the fear she absorbed for me and carried in private, all those terrible emotions she made space for in her own heart.

Justine is just an inch over five feet tall, petite in every way. Her soft voice betrays Midwestern roots with drawn-out vowel sounds and generous use of the word *gosh*. Gentleness and kindness are her most noticeable qualities, and yet on Thanksgiving night, this tiny woman was a valiant sentry, a brave guardian. She was a faithful friend to me.

And her watchfulness provided me a tangible picture of how the same God who calls himself a friend also calls himself a protector, both a shepherd who keeps watch and a gate that locks us into his refuge. Jesus called himself a gate and promised that anyone who goes through him would be cared for.[13] He didn't promise that we would be spared from death or hardship or intrusion, but that we, as his sheep, would find pasture in him.[14] And just as the Israelites painted lamb's blood above their doors when death invaded Egypt—just as Noah, his family, and the double-dating animal kingdom were declared safe once the door of the ark slammed closed—you and I are secure when cocooned in the belonging of our God.

I didn't really know how to pray for Mike through deployment. Sometimes I hummed or thought really hard and wondered if that was the same thing. Other times I clasped my hands or stared at the sky and inserted "Lord Jesus, I just pray . . ." every four or five words, really bringing my evangelical A game to the practice of prayer. And during those times I passionately asked that Mike would be protected and spared from death, that he would come home alive and with all of his limbs and without PTSD. I prayed that our marriage would stay alive too.

Jesus compared the exercise of prayer to knocking on a door and assured his disciples that if they were consistent in their knocking, the door would swing open to them.[15] I realize now that when I've been afraid, both back then and even now, I tend to misunderstand the heart of this promise. In the knocking, I have assumed that maybe God is inviting me to strive, to earn, to attract his attention that would otherwise be directed somewhere else. I have misunderstood prayer as a way to control God rather than a pathway of surrender to him. So naturally I found that knocking and banging and begging for assurances of Mike's safety didn't really bring me any peace at all. It felt like clamoring for control, pitching to God my best-case scenarios, micromanaging his provision, and then waiting for his compliance. I suppose I prayed this way because I worried that disaster might come on account of me if I didn't pray hard enough against it, as if a lack of spirituality might put blood on my hands or the whole world might fall to pieces if I didn't dictate to God exactly how he should hold it together.

But do you know what happens to a sheep when she tries to take over as shepherd? She wanders off, only to discover how profoundly she requires rescue. What the sheep needs is not more bravery or smarts or jurisdiction over the pasture. She needs to trust in the capability of her shepherd. She needs to believe that he is good.

The thing about fear is that it tends to unearth what you believe about God. Because each time you go knocking in prayer, your disposition will reveal your expectation of what's behind the door. Is it a sullen judge? A fickle benefactor? Is anyone there at all?

If you fear condemnation, then you will approach the door nervously, frantically, with a plea bargain in hand. If you believe God is absent or distant, then you might not bother knocking at all. And if you believe that God is only as good as your circumstances, then your prayers will become an itemized wish list, a queue of good gifts you're still waiting on but feel entitled to.

However, if you actually believe that God is both real and good, that you are completely forgiven, adopted, and loved—well, then you might knock on the door with the confidence that peace lives inside. You might see the door as a passageway that invites you in. And you might pray not just to ask for something, but to be with someone, because his presence meets the ultimate need you didn't even know how to ask for.

Of course, as Mike's mom, Katie, once told me, peace is its own kind of warfare. She said this to me over the phone after I confessed to her that I thought the deployment would be different, that I thought *I* would be different in the midst of it. I thought that since I knew Jesus, I would arrive at serenity faster, that I would inherently have more optimism instead of this abiding brittleness. I thought that trusting God would be so much easier, that faith would cushion this experience with pleasant feelings. What was shocking to me was how much energy it took to marshal my own mind, to redirect it away from imagined doom and toward hopeful trust. I wasn't even trying to arrive at full-blown optimism, necessarily, although that would have been nice. I was simply trying to function, to get on with it, and the act of putting one foot in front of the other was far more work intensive than I expected it to be.

Most mornings I woke up and opened my Bible, reading verse after verse about God as refuge, strength, and shield, as the consummate force that drives out fear. And I wrote these verses down in my journal as if trying to etch them into my heart, as if each one were a discovered gemstone that I held up to God and asked, "Is this valuable to me?"

Peace, at least for me, wasn't a tidy epiphany. It wasn't a one-moment conversion or a before-and-after transformation. It was a pursuit, a struggle, a war. It still is—this recurring choice to be ruled either by imagination or by what is true. That's what makes the pursuit of peace so tedious at times, when the only way to embrace it is to sort it through thought by thought, verse by verse, day by day; to take each thought captive and hold it up to the light.[16]

It seems to me that peace apart from deep conviction is a sort of delusion—a mind trick you play on yourself or a form of subtle denial. To survive deployment, I figured I could either delude myself into thinking the worst wouldn't happen or anchor myself to the belief that God would be a good shepherd to me even if it did.

Honestly? I clung to a little of both.

It was when I was home alone as a kid that I memorized a verse that has stuck with me into adulthood. Proverbs 3:25-26 (NIV) says, "Have no fear of sudden disaster or of the ruin that overtakes the wicked, for the LORD will be at your side and will keep your foot from being snared." I remember speaking this under my breath while standing at the door with heart racing. I remember shouting it into an empty, echoing house while I ran to the kitchen to get a pencil for my homework. Over and over again I recited it, as if I were speaking to the devil himself, intimidating him with a bigger weapon, a sword of truth.[17] Still, I don't remember exactly when I stopped being afraid to stay home alone, if the fear ebbed because I deliberately combated it with truth or if it simply faded as I grew up.

Even now, I'm not sure that fear is something we overcome altogether or if it's just an enemy we learn to battle more effectively. But I suspect that surviving times of heart-racing uncertainty involves some interplay between spirituality and practicality. You pray for God to increase your faith, knocking and knocking on the door, and then you choose to live as if he already has. You wake up in the morning, turn the blinds to let the light in, and walk out the front door.

# CHAPTER SIX

# MAKING ROOM
## On Homecoming

*It's a funny thing about comin' home.*
*Looks the same, smells the same, feels the same.*
*You'll realize what's changed is you.*
BENJAMIN BUTTON in *The Curious Case of Benjamin Button*

Reunions are exquisite when experienced in the third person. But they are surprisingly awkward when encountered in the first.

I've attended dozens of deployment homecomings as a friend, supporter, or spectator. An enormous American flag hangs in a gymnasium or aircraft hangar or waves from the clamped edge of a crane at the edge of a sports field. Men stand with hands in pockets or arms locked across their middles. Women shift their weight from side to side, regretting the choice to wear high heels for an occasion that involves so many hours of waiting. Each outfit is carefully curated, usually boasting some combination of red, white, and blue. Little girls have ribbons in their hair, and little boys wear brown belts with khakis already dirtied at the knees. I cry when I see really young babies, knowing that this moment is the first time they are meeting their daddies.

The estimated time of arrival is usually delayed fifteen minutes at a time for several hours until suddenly a bus turns the corner and everyone starts to scream. There is jumping and shrieking as the crowd pushes toward the front of a line held steady by Marines. Once the returning troops exit the bus, they often line up in formation, one by one, in rows of stiff-lipped attention. Frantically, we scan their faces, looking for familiar features, identifying a destination to run toward when the holding line dissolves. Kids hold signs they made themselves: "We're proud of you, Daddy." "We missed you, Mommy." Over and over again the signs say, "Welcome home. Welcome home. Welcome home."

Then, in a moment, without knowing exactly who gave permission, everyone starts running. Grown men in uniform drop to their knees, hands stretched wide to catch running children. After so many months of battle, it's beautiful to witness a reunion so closely mirroring the posture of surrender. Knees to ground. Arms outstretched. Finally, a conclusion.

But for the spouse, the loved one, the family member, homecomings are a complicated experience. Somehow the euphoria is tempered when you are the one in uncomfortable shoes, waiting under an American flag and trying to remember how you most naturally say the word *hello!* Your whole world is changing all over again, and not only do you have to put on a brave face, you have to wear a dress with a tasteful hint of cleavage and also remember to shave your armpits.

If you are the person at the front of the receiving line, every conversation in the weeks leading up to homecoming begins with the same question: "Aren't you excited?" And the truth is that you're not excited at all. You're scared, nervous, and profoundly restless, biting your fingernails and cleaning baseboards in the middle of the night. But of course, in conversation you lie and say, "I'm totally excited! I cannot wait!" Behind the scenes, homecomings not only destroy your nail beds, they make a liar out of you too.

It was right before Mike came home that I realized I had learned to live completely without him. I had replaced broken appliances and troubleshot cable and filed our joint tax return. I sat alone at weddings and survived a Christmas emptied of tradition. I even left a colorful customer service review for American Airlines after I was stranded alone for two days in Dallas. For months, I had cultivated the skill of fierce independence, and now I wondered if the soft spots reserved for needing him were all callused over. In this new version of my life, was there still room for Mike?

The person I was closest to—my own husband—had

become a distant voice on the phone, a sender of e-mails, a memory I had polished over time. And finally, *finally*, I had adjusted to this arrangement. I slept in the center of the bed. I left the house without telling anyone where I was going. I started referring to possessions as "mine" instead of "ours." I felt newly independent in a way that made me feel proud, that made me feel whole, but that also made me feel guilty.

Why *wasn't* I more excited?

Homecoming is really only graceful in photographs or from the safe distance of the bleachers. A hard chapter is ending, but another one is beginning—one that threatens to be hard too, just in a different way. During the deployment, you notice the spaces left vacant in the Marine's absence. But in the homecoming, you suddenly notice the ways you've filled them in. To the Marine I say, "Welcome home," but what I really mean is, "Who have you become? And what are we now together?"

Mike returned from deployment thirty pounds heavier, all of it in steely new muscle. When he stepped off the bus, I ran across a crowded field and threw myself into his embrace. Instantly, he felt like a stranger. His circumference had changed, and it no longer matched my muscle memory. He took up more space than I remembered. His neck was wider, his arms heavier. Physically speaking, Mike had become a domineering fortress, an

impenetrable citadel, and when I hit his chest it was like
colliding with a pillar of concrete. I didn't close my eyes
when we hugged, because without seeing him I couldn't
be sure that I was hugging the right Marine. In fact, the
intimacy of that first touch was so unfamiliar that it felt
wrong, as if I were a married woman lingering in the
arms of a different man while everyone around me took
pictures.

Once we made it to our hotel, Mike fell asleep and
stayed that way for two straight days. He was feverish
and unmoving, a giant bear collapsed into hibernation.
I had reserved us an expensive room in La Jolla Cove
with an ocean view, thinking we would stroll around the
shops and have slow conversations over gourmet meals.
Instead, I sat alone at the hotel bar that first night, eating
peanuts and drinking chilled white wine while trying to
decide which was sadder: that I was alone at a bar or that
Mike was home and my circumstances remained largely
unchanged.

After the first night, I transferred our accommoda-
tions to a budget hotel up the road where Mike could
sleep in a bed that didn't cost so much. When he
finally arose, we went to a casual breakfast café, where
he ordered two huge entrées and easily finished them
both. Then, and only then, did we begin to talk. It was
as if he needed to first overcome overwhelming hunger
and exhaustion before any other needs could be met.
It seemed so shockingly primal to me that the three

things he wanted most were sex, sleep, and food, while what I craved was a touch of emotional intimacy, to feel known and cherished again. And, I mean, if we're getting specific, I also really wanted someone to take me out to sushi.

This is where it began, the realigning of our mismatched needs, the re-remembering how much space my husband occupied: shoes in the entryway, plates of food on the table, another body in the bed. Both of us wanted to return to the old normal, the familiar place we had been before. But there was no going back. There was only discovering a way to move on, a way to make room. Both of us had to relearn how to share a car, a bed, a checking account, to renegotiate what we "normally" ate for dinner. It's amazing how, after living on your own for a while, the addition of one single person can feel like a crowd. And choosing to understand the person you're making room for is the only way to build a home big enough for you both.

Mike brought home hundreds of photographs from Afghanistan. There were pictures of the Afghan soldiers he trained and the feral dog that followed his team on patrols; pictures of Marines delivering humanitarian supplies to schoolhouses; pictures of herds of sheep blockading dirt roads; pictures of Mike's corner of the tent carefully organized with care packages stacked neatly beneath the bed. In outdoor photos, the land looked barren and deserted, every natural landscape sepia toned.

There were videos, too, mostly of Mike and the other guys lifting weights, thrusting a loaded barbell from knees to shoulders to sky. In the background, hip-hop music raged while Marines cheered each other on in reps or speed or weight. A week after the homecoming, as we sat side by side watching those moving memories on a laptop, Mike halfheartedly apologized for the crude language. He explained that the team used these videos to check their form because there were no mirrors in the workout area. But after half an hour of watching sweaty dudes work out, I uncomfortably asked, "But . . . if you filmed so you could watch your form back then, why are we watching them now?"

It didn't occur to me then that photos and videos are really the only souvenirs that a Marine brings back from deployment. And since there are never really any winners or losers on deployment or even in war, it's difficult to validate the fact that you were there. For seven or eight or twelve months, you work sixteen-hour days and risk your life for the intangible cause of country so that eventually you can turn the job over to someone else in the exact same uniform, a mirror image. And this life-altering experience acts like a baton that goes round and round a racetrack without ever making it all the way home.

Here's what I misunderstood: Mike wasn't so much showing me pictures as he was making a case that the experience mattered. Each photo was an inquiry. And there were so many of them. If a picture speaks a thousand words and each warrior comes home with several hundred, then a meaningful part of their lives becomes too bulky to share, too long to condense, too hard to explain, especially when a wife like me looks at the first hundred photos and thinks, *I get it. It's cool, or whatever. But now you're home. Can't we just get on with it?*

Frame by frame, I was introduced to each person in the context of patrols and mealtimes and the tedious grind of months camped outside the wire. There were pictures of the squalid bathrooms, pictures of the fire pits where trash transformed to black smoke, pictures of the time their truck got stuck in the mud while they were patrolling the border of neighboring Pakistan.

That incident had a whole album dedicated to it. Mike showed me images of the sunken tires' tracks, the stagnant truck, the Marines trying to free massive tires from a vacuum of mud. As the glare of the computer screen illuminated his face, Mike explained that a solitary American patrol truck stranded in a war zone was an invitation for an uneven fight, like a shining spotlight in a land populated by moths. All night they waited to be towed out of the mud by another patrol truck. They dozed in shifts under the stars with fingers ready on triggers just in case combat came before rescue.

Now, seven months later on the other side of the story, from the comfort of my bed, I looked at pictures of Mike beside the truck. He was wearing Kevlar from shoulder to hip, gloves, and a helmet the color of sand. Lassoed across his waist was an automatic weapon. But what was most noticeable in all the images was the fact that he was *smiling*. And I could not reconcile the fear I felt in hearing the story and the thrill with which he recounted it. I couldn't reconcile the danger of the moment with the smile that revealed he actually enjoyed it.

As the story goes, the Marines waited all night for a fight that never came. Unknown to Mike, his mom was awake that night too. She was startled awake with the urgent and inexplicable prompting to pray against one word: *ambush*. So she did, completely unaware of her son's situation. I guess you could say that a battle really was waged and won that night, a more invisible kind, but not any less real.

Those were the sorts of stories everyone wanted to hear when Mike got home, the dazzling and suspenseful ones. They wanted to know if he had seen combat, if he had shot anyone, if he had killed anyone, and, if so, how it felt. Close friends and complete strangers asked if he was angry now, if he had PTSD, if he woke up in cold sweats. Mike returned home three weeks after Osama bin Laden was killed, and several acquaintances asked if he was the one who delivered the fatal bullet. Slowly, I would reply, "Mike is a Marine. Not a Navy SEAL. Like, he's in a different branch of the military." Blank stares confirmed what I was learning in bits and Mike was encountering in waves: Homecoming is fraught with misunderstanding for everyone involved. As a spouse, it's so difficult to make room, not only for a person you know, but also for the versions of them that you don't understand. It's a challenge to accommodate not only the person they were, but the person they are now, to allow for expansion, change, and growth you didn't see coming.

When Mike came home, he needed less: less technology, less conversation, fewer choices at the grocery store. The first time we went shopping together, he spent five full minutes in the frozen foods aisle calculating the price of peas per ounce. Later, he caught up to me at the checkout to replace the ones I habitually bought for a generic version that offered a ten-cent savings. When he came home, Mike became intensely committed to frugality and protein consumption and this new workout regimen called CrossFit.

But he wasn't the only one who had changed. I had taken my newfound independence and become a sort of self-assured leader. In his absence, I had chosen a church for us, established a new network of friends, acclimated to a city that was still new to him. For the better part of the year, I had also been a full-time vegetarian. And when I told Mike this in all seriousness, he laughed aloud.

Since home was a place we were both rebuilding, Mike wasn't the only one displaced. I was too. We were crowded, not just in our living spaces, but within ourselves: congested with untold stories and deferred hopes and unanswered questions. There was much we wanted to learn of each other and more we wanted validated within ourselves. I wanted to know what it was like to interact with the Taliban. He wanted to know why I had opened an Ann Taylor LOFT credit card. Both were difficult to explain.

In her book *Roots and Sky*, Christie Purifoy calls homecoming "a process rather than a moment."[18] You would think that homecoming is an immediate unification: two pieces clicking together like a buckle, like a snap, like a zipper. But the reweaving of unity is neither crisp nor instantaneous. It takes time, and most of all it takes space. And sometimes this means you have to let the distance between you sit empty for a little while. A pause. A breath. A hesitation. Until you know the next thing to say, the best way to listen. Homecoming takes longer than you expect it to, because true reconciliation is tender. It's delicate and it's deep. You cannot hurry it into some superficial charade—all smiles and small talk. You might begin there, but in order to progress you must find the fortitude to linger in the awkward silence, to think of questions you don't know the answers to, to listen as eagerly as you talk.

For us, coming home did not transpire across a field under an American flag on a day circled on the calendar, but in the weeks that followed: in the unremarkable moments of sitting at the table, riding in the car, walking the dog, doing the dishes. These were the ordinary occasions when we learned how to be together again, to let conversation unfold naturally, as if the warm familiarity of habit unwound us somehow. Slowly, we exchanged our stories, one by one, not in any particular order, but whenever the mood struck, when the timing felt right, when one of us felt ready or something triggered the memory: "This is what happened on Christmas." "This is what I ate on my birthday." "So when I bought the washer, the craziest thing happened." "Did I ever tell you about what happened when I lost my ID?" "This one time on a patrol . . ." "Let's talk about my new favorite television shows and why you must get on board."

After a period of accidental drifting or palpable distance, at the end of a deployment or simply at the end of a long day, when you realize your story as a couple isn't united or even shared, it seems that the best place to begin is in retelling it to each other. You may have been there physically, or not. You may have been there emotionally, or not. But a powerful way to come home to each other, I have found, is in asking to bear witness to the pieces of the story you may have missed. *Tell me again what happened. Tell me again how you felt. Tell me again what mattered to you so that by listening I can show you how much you matter to me.*

Some call that catching up, but in marriage it seems more significant, like you're rebuilding your life together, brick by brick, story by story, erecting walls around a place that you're both inside now, adjoining two histories by remembering them together. Sometimes, coming home to each other simply requires cultivation of curiosity for a person who is familiar.

Reunions are constantly occurring in marriage, little ones and big ones, louder at times and softer at others. A reunion waits on the other side of every misunderstanding and miscommunication, at the end of every day. Between us we have a thousand homecomings, a million different ways we say, "I do." And we reconcile, I think, not just by running toward each other but by drawing each other out. It's a practice, a habit. In order to come together, we must also make room. So we lean in and pause, draw near and retreat; we make allowances for each other's faults and pray for a more spacious cushion of grace. Push and pull, extend and retract—we follow the trail of a suturing needle that gently performs a small miracle.

It knits us back together again.

# CHAPTER SEVEN

# THE RICKETY TABLE

## On Building Community

> *Home is a place not only of strong affections, but of entire unreserves; it is life's undress rehearsal, its back-room, its dressing-room, from which we go forth to more careful and guarded intercourse, leaving behind us much débris of cast-off and every-day clothing.*

HARRIET BEECHER STOWE, *Little Foxes*

The project started out small. We were being sent from Yuma to San Diego, and after house hunting for weeks online, we decided to live in downtown San Diego in a tiny but conveniently located apartment. The unit was seven hundred square feet, and among other things, it lacked overhead lighting, cabinet storage in the kitchen, and a reserved space for dining. What it did offer, however, was a Starbucks located directly beneath us and an Italian sandwich shop across the street. I mean, what else could we need? Living in the city was both exciting and daunting, not only because it would mandate the mastery of parallel parking, but also because it required a severe downsizing in furniture.

With some creative staging, Mike and I figured the apartment had enough space for a small table three feet by five feet long, give or take. So basically a glorified desk with four stools around it. And instead of buying a table the way normal people would, Mike and I decided to build it with our own hands.

To say that this was a joint decision would be lovely but entirely untrue. Pinterest had just risen to popularity, and the ever-streaming queue of possibilities had taken over my entire life. Up until that point, I had no idea that nearly every product available for purchase could actually be made at home for basically the same cost and nine thousand additional work hours. I considered this a bargain. Strangely, Mike did not.

Hastily, I sold the large dining set we owned along with the sectional sofa and reappropriated the blank space in our living room for a construction zone. It's possible that Mike decided to help me build our small table only after I eliminated all other options.

In case you are wondering, no, we did not have many construction tools or any building experience. Also, I lacked the critical character traits of patience and long-suffering. But I was restless enough to eagerly swing a hammer or grip a power saw, and Mike was fresh off the heels of deployment, which meant that he was used to dealing with temperamental people handling dangerous weapons. I saw only pros.

The building process included Mike studying blueprints or researching power sanders or doing basic addition on scraps of paper. On our frequent trips to Lowe's, Mike spent hours measuring things while I spent a lot of time playing on the flatbed cart or buying snacks at the cash register. We made a good team, I thought, though I constantly wondered (and asked) what was taking so long. I was convinced our "small table project" could be casually completed in a single weekend. It took us two months.

Assembling the basic table frame was not all that difficult, but the actual tabletop was. It required clamps and axles we didn't have, so in addition to the time and money we had already spent, Mike and I drove eighteen hours back to Colorado so my dad could help us fuse it together with his fancy (read: necessary) construction tools.

My dad is an experienced and talented carpenter, so when I called to ask if he could help us with this "easy" and "small" construction project we were working on, he seemed a little skeptical. Nevertheless, he opened up the garage door and helped us clamp and seal the tabletop together, only once suggesting that perhaps we should have considered a higher quality wood before creating a tabletop out of planks that would almost certainly warp within a year or two. "It adds character!" I said.

Back in Yuma, Mike and I pieced our table together.

It looked beautiful: a rustic tabletop stained in a gray-brown wash supported by a thick rectangular frame painted crisp white. I stood in our empty living room, admiring our work, and then placed my hands on the small table, ready to have a quiet moment of transcendence where the table would be blessed and consecrated for good use. This was my moment to stand on achievement, or at least to lean against it with two hands.

The moment, however, was interrupted when the table began to sway against my touch. Confused, I applied light pressure a second time. Same thing.

The table we made was not actually stable. The part professionally assembled—the tabletop—was solid, but the frame was wobbly, swoony, prone to dancing with sporadic, awkward movements, like a suburban mom trying Zumba for the first time. After hours of work, a weekend road trip to Colorado, and more money than it would've cost to purchase a nice, hard-to-assemble IKEA table, we had built a rickety one for ourselves.

Frantically, Mike retraced each step of assembly, double-checking that we had applied due diligence. We went back and forth to Lowe's, asking for brackets to fortify the joints and any other ideas that could resuscitate this table from the brink of failure. Nothing worked. The table swayed. And we weren't even as worried about the table collapsing as we were about dinner guests misunderstanding the sway as an earthquake.

Remember, we were moving to southern California.

And now the only furniture left to move was a single rickety kitchen table, the small project that had accidentally turned into one large undertaking.

The summer we moved to San Diego, I felt out of place in a big city where everyone seemed to have already met her best friend. One of the perks of living downtown is that you have access to restaurants and shops. The busy, unfolding world is visible through your living room window. But one of the downsides of living downtown as a newcomer is that every time you look out the window you see the entire metropolis's social life in bloom. I imagine that this is what it might have been like to be a solitary creature near the on-ramp of Noah's ark. You are fine with your temporary solitude until you notice that literally all the other pedestrians are traveling two by two.

Out my apartment window in the morning light, I watched business professionals on their cell phones walk into Starbucks and leave carrying maxed-out coffee carriers with both hands. I understood this as evidence that no one in San Diego drank coffee alone except for me. At lunchtime, women in maxi dresses and aviator sunglasses casually crossed the street in tidy groups of two or four, laughing over their shoulders while their long, wavy hair fluttered in the wind. I understood this to mean that the women in San Diego were already organized into adult sororities that I had not yet been invited into. How does one rush for such a thing?

I observed the social landscape mostly from my window while wearing pajamas, but occasionally I collected this data firsthand, outdoors as I walked my dog—still in pajamas. So you can understand how the barometer of my social awareness reached combustible levels. Alone, unemployed, and perpetually underdressed, I started to feel a bit panicky, like a loner in a group of people that had already partnered up.

Where Yuma felt desolate and sparse upon arrival, San Diego felt oversaturated in just about everything. People. Traffic. Shopping. Noise. The ocean was visible from almost everywhere, all geography oriented by seashores fringing bottomless seas. I had never seen a wider horizon in all my life, especially at sunset when the sun dissolved into water that stretched beyond the edge of the world. Everything about San Diego seemed to allude to abundance. Lord knows that the cost of living there required such a bounty. So I thought that surely here, out of the surplus of potential, we would find our best life. That's the carrot that dangles above every new address, isn't it?

In Yuma, I complained about its smallness, about living in a virtual fishbowl, about the guarantee of running into someone I knew while waiting in line at the pharmacy, red-nosed and miserable with a handful of soggy used tissues. I complained that there were too few places to eat, to shop, to explore. But just because San Diego was the opposite didn't mean it eliminated restlessness. Abundance, it turns out, is its own sort of problem.

There are cities in which it's easy to connect and cities in which it's easy to consume. Yuma was one. And soon I realized that San Diego was the other. I won't go so far as to say this is true for everyone, but I found that in a city like San Diego, with so much to offer, there tended to be a lot of social activity without a lot of social depth— a lot of side-by-side activity without a lot of face-to-face connection. Everyone was in a hurry. They already had plans. They dressed so much better than I did. And to get to someone else's house required a road trip involving four major highways, the risk of sitting in an hour of traffic, and the use of gasoline that temporarily peaked at $4.61 a gallon. Isn't it just easier to meet at a restaurant? To try to rendezvous at the beach? Or to just follow each other on Instagram?

In a city with so many options, it seemed like it should have been easier, or maybe faster, to arrive at meaningful relationships. But what is wide also tends to be sort of shallow. That is, with the exception of the ocean. And maybe that's why I expected so much from San Diego— both depth and breadth from a city that quite literally offered the sea.

However, in the buffet of social opportunity, you know what I missed about Yuma? Gathering around

someone's table. I missed having a narrow pool of
people to find friendship among. At least there I knew
where to begin, whom to introduce myself to first.

I missed building friendship slowly, organically, on the
foundation of mutual boredom, on the lack of better
plans, on the assumption that relationship was a form
of resourcefulness in itself, an end rather than a means
to a more interesting activity. Maybe this is why such
good friends are made in small towns or niche circumstances or tiny pockets of subculture. You have a nar-
rowness to speak from and live out of.

Smallness means you have a context from which to
begin.

After a decade of service, my friend Jill's husband
recently transitioned out of the Marine Corps. One of
the notable differences in building relationships outside
of the small military community, according to Jill, is that
you lose a common language to talk about your personal
life. There aren't as many overlaps of shared experience
to launch into discussions of marriage and family and
career. Conveniently, the military provides a vocabulary
for a common set of crucibles: deployments, transience,
and homesickness. Each is a pocket from which to dig
out conversation.

For example, in the military we can talk about the
difficulty of marriage by easily engaging in a discussion

about how we navigate the logistics of long-distance relationship. We can discuss the hardship of parenting in the context of transitioning kids to a new school or raising them far from family, since all of us are living as local transplants. And when we want to talk about lack of purpose, it's not a hard topic to bring up. We use the story line of fighting for career continuity between duty stations, since at any given time half of us are looking for jobs. We can talk about any one of a dozen topics and respond with something as simple as "It's so hard, isn't it? I've been there too." And that's the small beginning, the gentle buzz of resonance that confirms you aren't alone. Shared empathy might be the most fertile ground from which a friendship grows.

I'm not saying that everyone in a small community is naturally compatible, but smallness seems to breed commonality, and commonality helps us cut to the chase, particularly when we are personally familiar with the heaviness borne on the shoulders brushing ours. It's a lot easier to come out of hiding when you're talking to someone who has been through something similar, who you're pretty sure can understand. And isn't that what we're all looking for? A set of people, a tribe, a home team that gets it, that *gets us*? Because deep down we know that as uncomfortable as it is to let our imperfections show, those ragged edges are intended as connective tissue, like a rickety table that is best braced by bodies seated around it.

Our dear friends Dave and Arica were the very first people to dine at our rickety table. They flew into San Diego from Colorado with bathing suits and sunscreen, and we took them on a whirlwind tour of our new city—first to Coronado Island, then to Balboa Park and Old Town and Seaport Village. When we ate out, it was fish tacos and brewery burgers, followed by trips to Pappalecco for Nutella gelato. We were so efficient in our tour guide abilities that by the second day all of us were tired and sunburned and agreed to spend the second half of the weekend eating in.

So instead of languishing in the largeness of our city, we spent a lot of time in our small apartment, talking around our small table.

I know the ricketiness of the table shouldn't have mattered—especially to friends that we had known for so long. But on the first night we all gathered around for dinner, I wasn't as concerned about the temperature of the food or the topic of conversation as much as the movement of everyone's knees and elbows. I hoped those bony parts wouldn't bump the rickety parts. When anyone reached for the salt, I watched the water slosh in glasses. I even provided the unsolicited explanation that we were unable to serve steak because the collective back-and-forth motion of steak knives would certainly collapse the dining surface before anyone arrived at bite-size pieces.

I liked what the homemade table implied about Mike and me: that we were industrious, hardworking, creative artisans. But I was most comfortable discussing the finer details of our handmade furniture from the stability of our store-bought couches or, better yet, abstractly over the phone. As soon as we sat down for dinner, though, it seemed like the ideals the table stood for didn't matter because the table wasn't very good at standing in the most literal sense. It wasn't very good at being a table. While the vulnerabilities were most charming in narrative form, in real life they were distracting, uncomfortable, and slightly embarrassing.

Often, this is how I think of moving and starting again. In theory, it seems so charming to transplant an old life to a new place, as if quality of life hinges on a change of scenery or a larger backyard or a house with a respectable pantry. In narrative form moving can seem so adventurous, so romantic, the cure to a thousand problems. But the actual execution of it is, well, sort of clunky, namely because there is a mandatory transition phase at the beginning where you will stand out as an outsider. What I mean is that your adjustment may begin with lots of mistakes. You may learn a city first by all the things you get wrong about it. Names you misremembered, directions you thought you knew, parking tickets you were awarded for never having heard of a thing called "street sweeping." Maybe you adjust to new places with the poise and grace of an Olympic ice dancer, but the curve of my adjustment period lingers in the stage I've affectionately titled *Looking and Acting like a Fool.*

When Arica and Dave came to visit, I was still very much in this phase, a tour guide who smiled a lot but had no idea where she was going. So the impulse to overexplain the fragility of our table permeated more than the table. I felt the urge to explain away the feeble parts of our transitioning life, like the fact that we were still searching for a church, still looking for local community, still using the GPS to make it to the grocery store. We were in progress, at all points still freckled with imperfection. From a distance we may have appeared beautiful and stable, polished and whole and photogenic, but up close we were quaking under the weight of starting over.

But do you know what good friends do in this situation?

They eat with you anyway. They move with your sway. They ask the question beneath the question, not just "What's new?" but "How are you feeling about it?" They chase the heart of the matter, which is another way of saying *they chase and find you.*

It's not that Dave and Arica said anything to quell my insecurity about the table. Or maybe they did and I don't recall. But what I do remember is that they carried on around the table and through our lives as if the ricketiness didn't matter, as if it didn't offend or distract them, as if they didn't come to audit our adjustment or experience the largeness of our city or be impressed by the sturdiness of our newly remodeled life. They came for something so much smaller.

Us.

They came just to be with us.

And that's the narrow space where home is experienced in relationship—the place where you are known and loved at the very same time, even with all your rickety bits and "I don't knows" and accidental parking tickets. The place where you are seen and understood and not thought too much of. We all need people like this every place we are. This I know to be true.

Arica and Dave left on an early flight back to Colorado on a Sunday morning. They are close friends that for now are not local, but their trip unpacked San Diego for us in a revelatory way. They showed Mike and me what we were essentially looking for in our new city: not an activity or a title or a community, not even a church or a neighborhood, necessarily. Those are all filters to get to the thing we wanted most. What we were looking for was a Dave and Arica, for friends who would sit with us in the center of our rickety life and call it valid, call it good.

They took a large city and reminded us how to make it small, reminded us that the point is not to arrive at something perfect or polished, but to be brave enough to attempt something personal. To try. To risk. To build.

# CHAPTER EIGHT

# THE MOST HOMESICK DAY

## On Church

> The church is perhaps one of the few places left where we can meet people who are different than we are but with whom we can form a larger family.
>
> HENRI NOUWEN, *Reaching Out*

Sundays are family days, the days where the rhythms of church and brunch and afternoon football ease you into rest before the workweek begins. Sunday is the brief intermission before putting on tailored pants, brushing your hair, and working for a vested 401(k). I would venture to guess that fewer people floss on Sundays than, say, on Tuesdays. But then again, I tend to forget to floss on Tuesdays, too.

On Saturday most people run errands. You go to the grocery store or Home Depot or the dry-cleaners so that on Sunday you can stay at home. That is, unless you are a parent of school-age children, in which case you probably spend Sundays carting children and orange slices around in an enormous SUV so you can cheer for stampedes of uniformed confusion. I mean so you can watch them play soccer.

Ideally, Sundays are when you allow your most authentic self to emerge and stick around, the self that wakes up slowly and lingers in faded sweatpants while you drink coffee from a favorite mug that has a picture of a cat on it. You don't even like cats, but you love this mug for reasons you cannot explain. It has a brown ring around the inside from overuse, a tattoo of affection.

Or on Sundays maybe you pad around the house in thick socks that were gifted to you as a white elephant from a coworker at an office Christmas party. They are truly horrible. And you know this. You laughed when you unwrapped them. You rolled your eyes with false annoyance. But now you wear them every Sunday with an untied bathrobe and wild hair that's matted on one side. Because it is Sunday.

Sunday is a day of rest, a Sabbath, and most of us only know how to relax in familiar places, around familiar people, doing familiar things. We sleep best in our own beds. We rest in the parameters of routine. So my theory is that if you want to know the most organic part of a person, ask them what they do on Sunday.

As for those who are displaced—traveling abroad or on the move—it's difficult to return to familiar places when you are living somewhere new. Most of us don't know how much we miss home until we have to find a new routine for Sunday. And that's why Sunday isn't just a Sabbath. It's also the most homesick day of the week.

When I first moved away from Colorado, I couldn't call home on Sunday without getting a lump in my throat. My mom or dad or sister or brother would answer and my voice would quiver, nearly quaking with home-sickness, as if I didn't know how lonely I was until the moment a voice on the phone confirmed that my family was very far away. Often I would call when the rest of my family was still engaged in the routine I had left behind. They would have just finished eating lunch, or depending on the season, watching Broncos football in between sporadic couch napping. To this day, my mom makes box brownies in the red pan on Sundays, and I promise you that no brownies from any other place on any other day taste the same.

If I was home on Sunday afternoons, my mom, my sister, and I would run to Marshalls and complain about the size of our thighs over the high walls of the dressing room stalls. My mom would try on one hun-dred things and buy nothing. Rachel and I would have long discussions about exactly what caliber of blouse warrants forty dollars. The answer is none, unless it is miraculously slimming or almost our birthday or encountered at the end of a very bad week. When I'm

not in Colorado, my mom and Rachel still answer
the phone from Marshalls. I can picture exactly where
they're standing, near a full-length mirror under a fluorescent light at the end of an aisle, holding a shirt up
at eye level, with a free hand keeping the cell phone to
one ear. From a thousand miles away Rachel tells me
she can't find anything that fits; my mom says she's trying to convince Rachel to get "the cutest boots." Both
tell me they wish I were there.

"You have no idea," I say. "I do too."

Sometimes, even now, the lump in my throat returns,
but usually it only happens when I need to go shopping
for cute boots, when a holiday celebration is near, or
when I am at the end of a very bad week.

Those phone calls are like peering into a window
that displays exactly what I am missing. They are hard,
yet now they have become part of my Sunday routine.
Because if the choice is between calling home or not
going home at all, I choose the phone call.

I choose the window, even if I can't walk through
the front door.

Even from far away, Sundays are when I want to
retrace the habits of my upbringing, to be steeped in
familiarity, to occupy the seat at the table that is reserv-
edly mine. On Sundays I want to feel like a native, like
a local, to find respite from the foreignness of the outside world. I want to retreat to familiar territory, to be
around family, to be fed and provided for, to eat five

brownies straight from the red pan without an ounce
of self-consciousness. Around the table, I'd like to have
conversations completely prompted by the phrase
"Remember that time . . . ?"

On Sundays I don't want to explain myself, you know?
I want to already be known.

Perhaps this is why I put so much pressure on church,
because church services are usually held on the day I'm
looking for people and places and things to satisfy this
insatiable longing for home. On this Sabbath day, I want
to be around family, since this is the only place I know
how to rest.

This struggle for rest has been a recurring theme
in my life. Specifically, I've never been very good at it.
I have memories from middle school of reading a book
until 4:00 a.m. and then going into my parents' room
and whispering, "Mom! Dad! I'm still not tired." They
would respond with a groan that I can only assume was
an expression of deep gratitude for having me.

My insomnia became extra problematic in middle
school, when sleepovers were the currency of social accep-
tance. I loved sleepovers, but only between the hours of
6:00 and 10:00 p.m. As soon as the first person confessed
they were tired, the slow betrayal began. Other girls would
curl up in sleeping bags or pull their side of the covers
up from beneath the canopy of a living room fort. And
I would start to panic. When the darkness came and all
the others knew how to go to sleep, I felt abandoned,

alone, wild with wakefulness in an unfamiliar house that
had weird sounds and usually a blinding red light from
an overhead smoke detector. I could not rest in a foreign
place.

Inevitably between 11:00 p.m. and 1:00 a.m., I would
find a phone and call home. My dad would answer the
phone with a "hello" slurred in sleep, unsurprised by the
call that occurred every time I tried to spend the night
anywhere else. As soon as I hung up the phone, I would
get my bag and wait by the door, nearly crying with relief
when I saw headlights coming down the street. As soon
as the car parked, I ran to the passenger door, waving my
thanks to the exhausted mother of the hosting friend.
The moment I got into the car, I was certain that the passenger seat was the safest, loveliest, most merciful place in
the whole wide world.

On the way home my dad would squeeze my knee
once without taking his eyes off the road, a single blinker
flashing loud in the silence of the car. His presence
brought a calm so palpable that often I would fall asleep
on the drive home, contradicting—and maybe even
healing for a moment—the insomnia that had raged like
a riot within me just moments before.

I suppose on Sundays, when I'm feeling homesick,
when I'm tired and restless and experiencing a sort of
daytime insomnia, I deeply want something like the
passenger seat of my dad's car, a gentle means of rescue,
a connector between lost and found, a vehicle for tak-

ing me to the place where I can finally rest. And over the years, I've found that usually I want that place to be church.

I don't know about you, but I have found that I don't feel settled in a new city until the Sunday routine is set. Usually that begins with looking for a new church, which is remarkably similar to dating—it's awkward and self-conscious and you're never quite sure if you're dressed appropriately.

At first you check out a church anonymously, sitting in the back and adamantly *not* filling out the newcomer card or raising your hand when the emcee invites you to be recognized. You do *not* want to be recognized.

After a positive first impression, the church and you might grab a drink—a free coffee available in the lobby, next to the smiley volunteer passing out bulletins. The bulletins are also free, as are the smiles, so this church is basically a jackpot of generosity. You like this.

And because good Christians fall in love under the oversight of half a dozen chaperones, the next natural step in your relationship is regular attendance at a small group (also known as a life/cell/connection group). This happens on weeknights at someone's house around a coffee table where chips and salsa are all but guaranteed.

If things continue to go well, depending on the denomination, you attend a membership class. This is the promise ring of the relationship. It's around this time that you start to tell your parents about the church. You tell them about the people whose names you have memorized and the pastor who teaches very well even though he begins too many sentences with "On this journey called life . . ." Your parents are thrilled you are settling down with a church and starting to think about making babies. I mean disciples.

After a whirlwind romance and a few fights over doctrine, theology, and/or the loudness of the music, you decide that this is your church. You enter into a contract, become a member, and agree to open up your life and your free time and, terrifyingly, a portion of your bank account to a community of people who promise to become your family.

In my experience, church commitment is generally followed by a honeymoon period where all seems right and well. That is, until you realize that every human relationship, including those within the church, is imperfect and sort of weird. Sometimes even disappointing. Often, there are things you would change, some details about the service order or song choices that you wish more closely resembled the church you grew up in. But you realize that the only way to survive homesick Sundays is to find family in each place you are. In order to survive a life on the move, you must create a form of stability on Sundays. And the moment a church becomes this place, you upgrade its name with an important adjective, a moniker that makes all the difference.

You call it your *home* church, not because it's perfect, but because it's where you decide to become a regular on Sundays.

It seems to me that the good news of the gospel gets even better for those on the move, because God gave us family that traverses geography, a community of people that all call the same person Father. So now every place I go, I know that if I look hard enough, I can find siblings nearby. Conveniently, many of them congregate at churches on Sundays. Church, then, becomes an orienting landmark to find the family I haven't met yet on the day I need them most.

On each new set of orders, we have settled at a different sort of church. In Yuma, we went to a midsize church that was older and a little sleepy. The first service on Sunday mornings was called the "traditional" service and featured a choir of white-haired adults who could sing any hymn in three-part harmony. The second, "contemporary" service had an electric guitar and a worship leader who wore jeans and flip-flops. About seven people raised their hands during worship in this service, which was perceived as an act of radicalism. It wasn't the Sunday morning services, necessarily, that Mike and I loved about that church. It was how much we trusted

the pastors and how much we loved our young-adult
small group that met on Wednesday nights, with potluck
dinners of Oreos, chips, and stale brownies that some
young Marines' mothers sent them in the mail. We were
all in our early twenties then, and we sat on the floor in
a circle on Wednesday nights, wrestling with the truth of
who Jesus is, who we are, and why the intersection of the
two matters.

When Mike and I moved to Athens, Georgia, for
a four-month training school, we went to a satellite
campus of a megachurch, where Christian celebrities
preached to us from a movie screen every Sunday. All
the young women, I noticed, wore cute cowboy boots
with sundresses, while the young men wore shorts in
pastel shades and hung sunglasses from elastic Croakies
around their necks. It was the South, ya'll. And during
those months we went to church anonymously, which
felt odd and hollow, like a house we regularly visited
without ever feeling at home, a Sunday habit we kept
purely on principle.

In a different city, we went for years to a church that
was eagerly charismatic, where praying wasn't praying
unless you paced the floor and talked fast, occasionally
in tongues. The pastor spoke loudly and animatedly,
preferred lots of lights and production, and always facili-
tated an extended altar call at the end of service.

On another set of orders, we went to a church that was
quite intellectual and talked an awful lot about theology

and "the elect." There were bagels in the foyer before each service, which was held in an elementary school gymnasium with folding chairs and curtains to cover the alligator mascot painted on the walls. This church was more intentional with relationships than any other we had attended. It was strictly no-frills, yet it managed to mostly land on the things that truly mattered.

Among these, there were churches we loved and one church experience that wounded us deeply, that made us wonder if it was time to divorce the whole thing, maybe spend our Sundays at brunch or in the outdoors or in bed. Honestly, for a while we did. We listened to sermon podcasts and watched worship on YouTube.

But while belief in Christ is surely a vertical relationship, it is a horizontal one too. None of us were adopted as only children. We were adopted in a crowd, in a pack, which means we have spiritual siblings all over the place. So even out of the disappointment and disillusionment rose the persistent, badgering heartbeat of family, of knowing there was somewhere we still belonged, of feeling that Sundays were family days that weren't intended for isolation. Family heritage isn't an easy thing to shake, as imperfect as it is.

My friend Kenra once told me that one of the ways Jesus was wise in establishing the church was that he knew it would be filled with broken and dysfunctional people, which makes the church itself often broken and dysfunctional. "But that way," Kenra said, "we can't worship the church. We can only worship Jesus. And church is where we go to worship him together."

If church is like family, then this much is true: It's not always easy. More often it's hard. My biological family, as beautiful and beloved as it is, has stumbled through divorce and consequent remarriages. We have gone through periods of fighting, of not talking, or periods where I talk to my sister about my brother or my brother about my sister. They annoy me. I annoy them. It's a whole thing. We have just as much sin and dysfunction as the rest. But still. But yet. But *family*. There's a catch there, don't you think? A loyalty that trickles through your blood and the connectedness of your history, something you can't quite explain. Maybe this sounds trite—please forgive me if it does—but I stick with church for the same reason I stick with my family. Without them, I'm an orphan, a runaway. Without them, I'm missing wholeness and complexity, history and heritage. Like it or not, they are the tentacles of who I am. Without them, there's no need to practice forgiveness or believe in restoration. Without them, Jesus becomes a small personal mascot instead of a unifier, a restorer, a mediator of relationship.

Without the fight for roots, I forgo them altogether.

In her book *Traveling Mercies*, Anne Lamott tells a story I love about a little girl who got lost in the town where she lived. The girl ran up and down the streets, looking for

anything she recognized, but grew more and more fright-
ened as her surroundings remained unfamiliar. Eventually
a police officer stopped to help her. The girl hopped in the
passenger seat of the patrol car, and the officer drove her
around town until she spotted a church. When the little
girl saw it, she said, "You could let me out now. This is my
church, and I can always find my way home from here."[19]

I'm not saying that a sense of home or adoptive family can only be established in the four walls of church.
Truly, it can happen anywhere. But when I feel displaced
in my surroundings, when I'm in a hurry to find stability
and I don't know where else to go, it is helpful to have
a set meeting place. And when we move to a new town,
feeling a bit like loners or orphans or vagabonds, when
I feel like a lost little girl, I long to have coordinates of a
place where I know family can be found, an address that
is easy to remember and identify.

So I suppose this is both a declaration and an
invitation—that family is worth searching for, worth
fighting for. And I go to church on Sundays now as a
vote of confidence, as a way of telling my soul that someday I will kneel beside siblings at the throne of heaven.
But until then I will show up on Sundays and help set
up chairs or pass out bulletins. I will commit to a local
church as a way of making my temporary geography
home. I will be reckless enough to hope, to set my alarm
on the last day of the weekend. On Sundays, I will start
at church as a place that helps me find my way home.

# CHAPTER NINE

# ALMOST THERE

*On Faith and Doubt*

*Life is always a rich and steady time when you are*
*waiting for something to happen or to hatch.*

E. B. WHITE, *Charlotte's Web*

I found out I was pregnant on a Monday morning.

The previous Friday night I had taken a test that came back negative, and I had believed it. Still, I thought it was strange that I felt like puking the whole time I drove to my friend Melissa's house. Driving north on Highway 163, I cracked the driver's side window and brainstormed the most rational places to vomit inside a moving vehicle. The cup holder? Out the window? Into my cupped hands? In addition to these nausea symptoms, I felt like napping in public places and being cruel to my husband 100 percent of the time.

This is not normal, since I never nap in public.

I found out I was pregnant when I was twenty-five years old, by all accounts a proper adult. I had a job and a husband who also had a job. Both of us had driver's licenses and were up to date on vaccinations and taxes and most current events. For the past four years, we had kept a dog alive, which seemed like it should count for something. We shared a car, a reasonable Honda that took basic unleaded fuel, so it seemed like a baby would be a completely rational addition to our very normal, nonfrivolous adult life.

But when the idea of a baby turned into the reality of a pregnancy, when the double blue lines proved that I was about to become an even adultier adult, I was stunned silent. Mike was in the other bathroom shaving before work when I interrupted him with an openmouthed gaze and extended to him the plastic evidence. We sat down on the bed and felt completely overwhelmed for a full ten minutes. Both of us cried silent tears without fully knowing why, as though our eyes needed to water in response to a life that was changing. It was changing for the better, of course, but even good change is scary change, especially when you aren't expecting it. My first questions were: "Are we even *allowed* to have a baby?" and "Does God know about this?"

The morning charged ahead anyway, and I had to blow-dry my hair and pour untouched coffee down the drain, two things I truly hate to do. We both went to work and sat at computers and wrote e-mails and

answered phone calls while sending each other the same
text message back and forth:

"Is this for real?"

"Is this for real?"

"Is this for real?"

Life changed so loudly that morning that I was sure
others must have heard it happen. But they didn't. No
one knew. So we carried the secret for a while. I took
bathroom breaks every nine seconds and ate like a person who had never experienced a carbohydrate before.

I was the pregnant one, though when we shared the
news with friends and family, the term became bizarrely
plural. *We* were pregnant, the two of us, together, man
and wife, an incubated union. Mike happily told people
that *we* were pregnant as he ate sushi, as he drank a cold
beer, as he fit into pants without a hint of elastic in the
waistband. In a benevolent gesture, he offered to keep up
with my weight gain in what we termed the "pound-for-
pound challenge." This plan, however, backfired as he
drank an inordinate number of protein shakes, worked
out harder and longer, and became more crisply muscu-
lar as I discovered the manifold ways a single person can
define the word *bloated*.

That summer we went to the beach often, and I
would sit in the sand and watch brave souls ride boogie
boards toward shore. Face-first they would lie on foam
planks, hands gripping the sides, faces a mixed display
of determination and confusion as they tried to interpret

the propulsion of the wave. And this is how pregnancy
felt to me, like the act of civilizing a wild wave. Certainly
I felt a distant sense of wonder, a levity in knowing I
was being carried somewhere important, but I was also
racing headfirst into the spray of uncertainty. I was holding tight and looking forward with eyes that betrayed
fear even as they recognized the thrill of hovering over
waters, even as they experienced a miracle in motion.

The first miracle I experienced as a child was the revelation that Jesus lived in my actual heart. My parents spoke
of Jesus in my heart, but I'm not sure they anticipated
how literally I would take the information. I understood
that the heart was made up of four chambers with a bonus
upper room, perhaps a renovated attic above the garage
where Jesus took up residence and could be seen through
an illuminated window as he worked by candlelight to
edit the entire Bible. When I got my first X-ray in the
third grade after an unfortunate bowling accident, I was
disappointed that the doctors decided to photograph
only my injured right hand instead of the entirety of my
body. If only they had X-rayed my chest cavity, too, I was
certain they would have encountered Jesus and likely gotten saved.

   To me, the presence of God wasn't just spiritual or
even ethereal; it was downright biological. From the
moment Jesus became my cardiovascular roommate,

I understood that I was no longer singular. There was an invisible *we* at play, a hospitality of the soul that interacted with the behavior of my body. I was a Russian doll that accommodated hidden iterations of life within, one wooden shell stacked upon another, a stand-alone number that secretly was a sum. I was a hollow container created for pouring out, for being filled, a structure built for occupancy. And so I suppose I've wrestled with the idea of hosting life within me long before that early Monday morning, long before I found out I was pregnant, and long before I recognized pregnancy as a metaphor for the spiritual state I was in all along.

When Jesus commissioned the disciples to a life of faith, he promised them that after he left the earth, the Holy Spirit would come in his place.[20] The Holy Spirit was a presence, a Spirit-life that would occupy the souls of those who invited him in. And from the inside out, the Holy Spirit would infuse believers with the same power that operated in Jesus, enabling them to live like him and for him. It would inspire behavioral change just as pregnancy gives women a nesting bug. But instead of cleaning floors and building cribs, Christians would be instinctually motivated to love God and love people, to serve them just as Jesus had.

What Jesus was really telling the disciples is that the life within would be constant and sure, an ongoing intimacy with God himself. So perhaps the greatest miracle of Jesus was not turning bread into wine or blindness into sight, but transforming everyday people into portable tabernacles, houses of God, enabling those who believe to become impregnated with the living Spirit of God.

It's rather fitting, then, that Jesus arrived on the scene by way of a surprise pregnancy. A virgin became pregnant and carried the life of God through the surprise of grace, not by any act she had done. And this was a forecast of what was to come for the rest of humanity. Jesus made us right with God so that we could be filled with his power, with his indwelling presence. In an act of extraordinary grace, God placed life within us.

To be honest, most of my pregnancy was spent convincing myself that it was real, not imagined, that I was growing a human, not an idea or an alien or a tumor. At doctor's appointments the obstetrician would confirm that there was, in fact, a baby growing inside of me when she'd press the fetal heart monitor against my belly and find the heartbeat. The sound wasn't a thudding or a pounding but a swooshing, like basketballs sailing through the net of a hoop, one after another. *Swish. Swish. Swish. Swish.* "See?" she would say. "That's the heartbeat. That's your baby." Mike would squeeze my hand and look at me with misty eyes, and we would be overcome with wonder, with something deeper than excitement. Love. Belief. Hope. I'd listen very hard to the rhythm, trying to memorize it, trying to empty everything else in my head so I could hold only that sound. And for that brief moment, I was so sure. I had evidence—if not something I could hold in my arms, then something I could hold in my head.

But in between doctor's appointments, I sometimes wondered if the baby inside me had died or evaporated or gone into hibernation. Of course, on the days I was riddled with discomfort I lamented the symptoms, but the days of profound silence were unsettling for a different reason. When there was no nausea or fatigue or when the baby wouldn't move much, I would be so casually contented that I'd forget I was pregnant. And this was amazing until late in the day when I'd remember I was carrying a human that I hadn't heard from in a while. Was she all right? Was this pregnancy still active? Viable? I would poke the belly and pray with an edge of anxiety. Should I call the doctor? Call a pastor? Go to the hospital?

When I wasn't sure what to do, I'd open my computer and read through pregnancy discussion boards where fellow mothers would tell me that my symptoms—or lack thereof—were either completely normal or indicative of impending catastrophe. I'd become convinced that years ago I should have started eating entirely organic or cleaning with only salvaged rainwater or stopped using microwaves. Mike would try to soothe me, first with words of assurance and sound logic, then with a smoothie. At the precipice of full-on panic, usually the moment I dialed the after-hours triage line, there would be a tiny rustling in my belly, a jab of an elbow or heel in my rib cage. Then: relief.

The life within me was consistent even when my awareness of it was not. It seems to me that to be pregnant is to learn the bravery of walking by faith and not by sight, which is a very hard thing to do.[21]

It is so strange to be pregnant, isn't it? To accommodate the presence of someone who is both stranger and kin, a tiny living paradox. At once this person feels foreign and familiar, both an intruder and a welcome houseguest. There were times that my relationship with the baby felt deeply intimate, when I felt overwhelming sensations of love. I thought of the baby often and marveled at the tangibility of her nearness—kicks and hiccups and somersaults. But then there were other times she felt distant, imaginary, cloaked in silence and mystery. I wanted to love my child with consistent emotion, but I found that I swung from sentimentality to indifference, from fear to euphoria to casual contentedness, every twelve seconds. Nothing really helped to stabilize the pendulum of emotion. Not even smoothies, which Mike obviously found frustrating.

Just as the emotionality of pregnancy fluctuated often, so, too, has the expression of my faith. There have been times when the presence of God has seemed so close, when I've gotten chills at hearing or reading a truth that rings as clear and right as a bell. I have sensed God during a conversation with a friend that is so timely and nourishing, it feels like a divine encounter. I have been certain of God within me while sharing insights that have never previously occurred to me, when the words that tumble out of my mouth are loaned, so clearly borrowed from wisdom I don't possess. I have sensed God in reading the Bible—verses jumping off the page, as if the act of reading is the same as listening to a booming voice speaking. Other times, I have sensed God in worship, when I can't even sing the words, can't even whisper them for the lump in my throat and tears on my cheeks, because surely there is a thickness in the air, a hovering over the deep that is in me and around me, a hurricane of peace and love and comfort that has wrapped around me like a blanket, swaddling each part of me. Sarah Bessey writes, "We have these moments of transcendence, like the veil between heaven and earth is fluttering, we can't breathe for the loveliness of the world and each other"—moments when our awareness of God "locks into focus."[22] These are the moments when God feels so extraordinarily personal, a family member, a friend. Being in his presence feels like coming home, and perhaps that's the point. Because that is what heaven will be.

But then there are other times when it seems that God is nowhere to be found, when I nudge and prod and pray and hear nothing, when I open my Bible and read words that feel stale, even as I know each word is true. There are times I try and try to forgive, to have a better attitude, to stop cursing or gossiping or envying what others have, and instead I just feel stuck. "I want to do what is good, but I don't. I don't want to do what is wrong, but I do it anyway."[23] I wrestle with imperfection, with sin, and in those times God seems like a stranger living within me, a roommate who is slacking on household cleanup.

Of course I realize that my sensory awareness of God is fuzzy and unreliable, similar to leaves and grass that wither and fade in season.[24] Surely the nearness of God's breath is proven through the Scripture it inspired, not just the sensations it provokes.[25] But in my most fragile moments, when I'm feeling needy or desperate and filled with doubt, there is a real desire not just to know God but to feel him, to experience the goose bumps or tears or a quickening of heart. There is a longing for something tactile to remind me that God is indeed alive in me, that he is near in a palpable way.

It seems to me that the Christian life—and the physical life too—is a lot like pregnancy. It's wrapped up in waiting. We wait on things like the birth of a child or the right job or friends or reputation. We wait to know where we are going next and for how long we will be on the move. It's especially in these times that we're eager to hear good advice or insight on what's to come. Friends and family may weigh in, try to encourage or commiserate. But really, I think, when life is in limbo, what we want is a reminder of cosmic control, evidence of a divine sovereignty at play. Some people get superstitious, looking for signs and omens. But beneath it all, I think what we are waiting on is the discernible voice of God.

It reminds me of when Elijah stood at Mount Sinai waiting to hear from God.[26] A windstorm passed by first, ferocious and mighty, but God was not in it. Then there was an earthquake. Then a fire. God was in neither. God was in none. Where was he? Was he even near?

Then, finally, maybe even at the precipice of full-on panic: a gentle whisper.

God spoke to Elijah, but only after Elijah waited, only after he wrestled with the weight of silence. It's almost as if the waiting were a form of preparation, a heavy expectancy that contextualizes what we long for most.

God never leaves us.[27] He doesn't run out for a latte or fall asleep at the wheel or duck out for a quick smoke break. He's ever present. Emmanuel. God *with us*. But I think he does keep us waiting. Sometimes he purposefully stays silent. And I don't pretend to know exactly why, but I suspect that it's a sort of refining moment that sharpens our resolve, that causes us to cling to his written Word and position our lives behind the promise that he is with us—even when we can't sense him. Frederick Buechner writes that engaging with the seeming absence of God is a sort of sacrament, "a door left open, a chamber of the heart kept ready and waiting."[28]

It is a silence that teaches us how to listen.

Waiting is best characterized by silence, isn't it? It is the bated breath before news arrives, the absence of information, the nerve-racking quiet before a knock on the door, before a telephone ring, before a guest of honor arrives. There is the long wait of pregnancy and then the brief wait of delivery that feels even longer: the moment a baby is born and you wait for her to cry.

The silence before the sound.

In the delivery room, Mike and I heard the voices of the doctor, the nurses, the medical assistants; the sound of the monitors beeping with my pulse—but those weren't the sounds we were listening for. Those didn't bring any rest at all. In fact, in the absence of the single sound we were waiting for was only unbearable uncertainty. Is she here? Is she okay? Is she alive?

Our hearts raced with anticipation. The silence was the sound of hovering dread and hopeful expectancy.

But then from the silence: an infant's cry.

Life within was now born.

Often the birth of a child, the birth of anything, really, is remembered as a simple sentimentality, a point of arrival. It's flattened to an experience of pure joy and revelation. Faith can be undersold like that too. A seeming destination rather than a slow process; a wrestling, a longing. But it's the waiting that shapes us. It tunes our ears and fixes our eyes, and if I had to take a guess as to why, here's what I would say: We learn to treasure most that which we have waited on.

Practically speaking, I've found there are moments of resounding satisfaction in the presence of God. There are snatches and whispers of certainty. And oh, how I long for those instances that confirm what I know to be true—that God is the ultimate source of peace and love, the home to my homesickness. Yet even as a person of faith, I still feel homesick sometimes. I'm chronically curious to find the place of *more*, or perhaps it's the place of *enough*. God satisfies, yes, but even so I tend to be restless by nature. Maybe it's because I've tasted and seen God in enough meaningful ways that I know there's more to him, and the suspense is killing me. Or maybe it's because I've found that home isn't strictly a place of geography or community or even elevated spirituality— it's a combination of them all. And only the voice of God can discern that interplay correctly, which makes it the thing I need the most.

The Bible tells us that the Holy Spirit within us acts as a foretaste of what is to come.[29] Like an appetizer before a feast, a preview before the big show, the Spirit "puts a little of heaven in our hearts so that we'll never settle for less."[30] So what if the longing for home and the presence of God are not two opposites but coexist as one phenomenon? God is among us, but he is also beyond us: relatable and relational, but also supreme. To put it another way, what if God is a source of rest and restlessness at the same time? Both satisfaction and suspense, a home here and a home still to come?

You and I are caught in the uncomfortable in-between. We seek and find, but mostly we wait. And in the waiting, all we can do is place our lives behind the promise that God is here with us, a home pointing toward a better home to come. We are restless because we're not there yet, but God's Spirit within us reminds us that we almost are.

# CHAPTER TEN

# WHERE OUR PARENTS LEFT OFF

*On the Pull to Move Back*

*I wish to thank my parents, for making it possible.*
*I wish to thank my children, for making it necessary.*
VICTOR BORGE

I think the biggest question of a transient life is "When will it end?"

When is it time to settle down? Buy a house? Put down roots? Move back home?

Many of our military friends, especially early on before any of us had kids, said they would continue this transient lifestyle up until the moment they became parents. Then, they said, they wanted to raise kids near family. Kids were always the game changer, it seemed. And if I'm honest with you, this notion seemed hyper-sentimental to me at the time, the sort of thing you're supposed to say whether or not you actually mean it, a habit of following tradition rather than your heart.

Back then and occasionally even now, I didn't consider it a hardship to live far from home. The notable exceptions were when Mike was gone for long stretches for work, when my brother had an extra ticket to a concert, or when I didn't feel like cooking dinner. So, by that description, I suppose I've missed home a lot. Because I am an uninspired cook, and my brother goes to concerts constantly.

But I have enjoyed the distance too. I like charting our own way. I like the independence of establishing ourselves in a city unfamiliar with our bloodline. I like encountering local restaurants and parks and churches with fresh eyes. And I like that we get to report back our findings to family when they come to visit. I value that we are the authorities on our town because we got here first. After a lifetime of being dutiful students and younger siblings, finally we get to play the teacher, the tour guide, the expert. Finally, we are the ones to ride shotgun.

But a few years ago something happened to complicate all of this.

I became a parent. First to a daughter, then to a son. And all of a sudden the ties that only loosely tethered me to Colorado violently retracted. I began to feel a pull, not just in a casual, holiday-airfare-is-expensive sort of way, but in a stop-everything-I-think-my-worldview-just-changed sort of way. I started saying the phrase "I want to raise kids near family" with actual, full-hearted conviction.

It's not just for the free child care, of course, although that would be really nice. And it's not because my mom tends to overbuy at Costco, although my empty pantry would happily remedy that situation. I'm drawn toward moving home now because I'm convinced that one of the best gifts we can give to our kids is exposure to our parents.

Isn't it true that we project our longings for home onto people as much as places? And maybe that's why as we get older, we miss our parents more.

When my in-laws come to visit us in San Diego, we sit around the kitchen table, talking for hours. They ask good questions, but more than that, they listen as if they aren't in a hurry. "Tell me about . . ." How do you feel about . . ." "What is going on with . . ." None of their inquiries can be answered mindlessly with a yes or no, so I answer in run-on sentences and stories from childhood that I only remember at exactly that moment.

Conversing with the DiFelices is like participating in an archaeological dig within yourself. Their questions act like gentle brushstrokes that help you unearth your deepest convictions so that you can finally say what you mean. To be around them is to discover the truest parts of yourself.

When my mom comes to visit, we move. I mean this

literally—we actually moved houses when she came to visit one spring—but I mean it generically, too. When she visits, we go on walks or go shopping or chase the kids around the backyard. She wears enormous orthotic walking shoes and her short hair in a ponytail as we move along the sidewalk and talk about life as it is and life as it used to be. She asks about each one of my friends, from preschool to present, and demands a full rundown of their family life, occupation, and perceived level of happiness. Also, she wants to know how their mothers are doing and if they still live at that address on Pilot Court where I used to have sleepovers on the trampoline.

I find that when my mom is around, I'm my most unguarded self. I tell my bluntest jokes. I give my curtest answers, sharpest opinions. I tend to be more sarcastic and goofy—an unpolished version of my regular self. Stubbornly, she loves me anyway. So for better or for worse, when she comes to town, I sometimes act like a child because she is so good at being my mom.

All of our parents live in Colorado. They occasionally come to babysit their grandkids, using frequent-flier miles and the guest room that waits for them in our new house. They come to San Diego. We go to Colorado. There is always a "next visit" on the books, and, of course, there is always FaceTime. For now, this is what it looks like to remain close to family that lives far away.

Mike gets new military orders every three years or so,

so it's about on that rhythm that we routinely ask the questions "How long will we keep doing this? When is it time to move back home?" We tally the cost of transience and ask ourselves, "Is this worth it?"

For example, we consider that if Mike stays in the military long enough to secure retirement (a full twenty years), our daughter would be entering high school and our son would be in middle school by the time we moved back to Colorado. And that means that during their younger, more impressionable years, the years they have the free time and interest to spend time with extended family, they wouldn't have easy access to them. I'm not saying this is a bad thing, necessarily. I'm just not sure it's the best thing, either. You know?

There's the fact that I want our kids to be friends with their cousins. Not just see-you-at-Christmas friends, but the sort that play in the same intramural soccer league on Saturday mornings—the sort that pass on hand-me-down jeans and outgrown bicycles and the occasional seasonal cold. Maybe this is nostalgia talking, or exaggerated idealism. But what if it's not? What if this is something more valid?

Before becoming a parent, being settled was a desire but not necessarily an urgent necessity. It seemed like a reality that waited for me in the future, on the other side of the adventures I had to experience first. From that point of view, home was the place where you slept and showered, where you changed your clothes or did laundry or quickly tuned up your life so you could live it elsewhere. Work, for the most part, was an activity outside the home. You went home only to rest.

But when kids come along, even if you continue to work outside the home, the inside of the house becomes a place of work too. It's where you change diapers and give baths and make meals that can be strewn over the edges of place mats before hustling the kids, kicking and screaming, to an eight o'clock bedtime. It's where you wake up before sunrise even on the weekends; where you run around the house playing hide-and-go-seek for the millionth time; where you load and unload the dishwasher, the clothes washer, the dryer; where you nurse a baby; where you enforce time-outs and wonder if they're even working. Parenthood might be the most meaningful work of our lives, but it's also the most exhausting. So it becomes harder to neatly sort work from rest. The two commingle together like piles of unfolded laundry.

Maybe that's why I transpose my need for rest onto my parents, especially after becoming a parent myself. I know this isn't the case for everyone, but generally (and ideally) speaking, our parents should be a place to let our guard down. And the perk of living near them is that they can offer rest of the physical kind—by taking the kids for an afternoon and feeding them sugar I have expressly forbidden. Or they can provide rest in a different way: by watching as I raise my kids and regularly saying, "Honey, you're doing just fine."

I don't know about you, but here in the weeds of early parenthood, I'm loaded with good intentions and pangs of guilt and absolutely no idea what I'm doing. I'm self-critical and uncertain a lot of the time. But the hope is that our parents, now grandparents, tend to be different. Not always, but ideally, they are lighter now, full of grace and seasoned perspective. They have a life-long narrative that proves how tenderly the years redeem what makes the days long.

And I need that counterbalance sometimes.

Actually, who am I kidding? I need it all the time.

There are some families in the military who want to stay in the mobile lifestyle for a patriotic lifetime. There are others who count down the days until they can get out of the circus and move home. And then there are people like Mike and me who really love the military, really want to move home, and cannot, for the life of us, decide what is next or what is *best*.

The longing for home pulls more strongly some times than others. There are times stability sounds like relief, like rescue, and other times it sounds like gated boredom. The urge to move back comes in waves, in seasons, sometimes as a passing craving and other times as a desire so sweeping I'm not sure how I'll get through one more weekend, one more holiday, one more twenty-four-hour stomach bug without family nearby.

Mike and I don't have an answer yet of when it's time to move back home. So in the meantime we sit around the dinner table and have long conversations, unpacking life and ourselves in the way Mike's parents taught us. Each time we move, we unpack boxes quickly and meet neighbors as if they're long-lost best friends, because my parents showed us how to do that. In fact, just recently my mom met half the neighborhood before I found the box with pots and pans. And it was in the cab of a moving truck with my dad years ago that I saw my first shooting star. He and I looked up at the sky together and took it as a promise of God's faithfulness, even as we traveled toward the unknown.

We all are our parents' children at the very same moment we are our most independent selves. And I suppose that sometimes we have to miss our parents to realize how deeply we love them—and still need them.

For now, Mike and I have the pride of independence. We have the hustle of travelers who still know, deep down, there is really no place like home. We have the kitchen table and the sidewalks and the moving trucks, the familiar sites where we were shaped into being. And in the moments we feel lost or displaced, we return to those places to feel near to the ones we love, to pick up where our parents left off.

# CHAPTER ELEVEN

# OUTPOST

## On Hospitality

*Having guests and visitors, if we do it right, is not an imposition, because we are not meant to rearrange our lives for our guests—we are meant to invite our guests to enter into our lives as they are.*

LAUREN F. WINNER, *Mudhouse Sabbath*

Each new town acts as an outpost of home. The address changes, along with the climate and how said climate affects the volume and consistency of my hair. In Southern California, finding curbside parking on a whim, even in a neighborhood, is not as simple as you might think. In Yuma, there is plentiful parking downtown, though there is also a man who uses the landscaped medians to park and tie up his two pet donkeys.

So, you know, every place is different.

"Each place has elements of home," my former neighbor Michelle once told me. We met her and her husband, Ben, over the edge of our backyard fence when we moved from our urban apartment to a more suburban part of San Diego. On the day of our meeting, Michelle, Ben, and their kids were playing in their backyard. Mike, Molly, and I were playing in ours. We saw one another. We waved. And within an hour, Michelle had invited us over for dinner, Ben had thrown a ladder over the fence, and we had climbed over it, balancing a bottle of wine in one hand and Molly in the other. Our families became easy friends. And as is so annoyingly common in the military, Michelle and her family moved two weeks later.

This house is the first one we've had with a backyard. In it, Molly has a plastic playhouse with a red door that swings open and shut, windows with blue shutters, and the lurking presence of an innocuous spider that somehow manages to discreetly spin webs in the upper rafters without ever being caught. This spider is Mike's nemesis, but also his greatest fear, so the mounting battle between the two of them is continually postponed.

The backyard is where we spend most of our time—sitting on the porch, begging Molly to stop feeding the dog rediscovered goldfish crackers. Occasionally we even gather around the outdoor chiminea for a bonfire when the San Diego temperatures drop to a bitter sixty or, dare I say, fifty-five degrees.

When friends come over, almost always with their kids, we host them in the backyard. We sit around the patio table and eat food hot off the grill. If our guests are visiting from out of town, they always, *always* com-

ment about the perfect climate, about how it's so warm
and beautiful here and how maybe they should move.
Mike or I respond with vague agreement but also with
a word about the traffic, the parking, the cost of living. We say San Diego is great, but Colorado is better.
Discussion ensues.

Then when the sun goes down, Mike turns on the
large-bulb twinkle lights strung along the beams of the
patio. With filthy bare feet, kids run in and out of the
house, ketchup still smeared across chins and checks.
They always leave the screen door open, and this drives
me crazy. Flies sprint through their gaping opportunity,
as does the neighbor's cat. One child inevitably struggles
to transition the toy baby stroller she's pushing up the
step from outside to inside. She screams in frustration,
rages against the handles, until one of the parents gets
up to help her, lifting the front wheels up and over. The
stroller is occupied with a large stuffed bear, four dead
leaves, a sock, and a half-empty sippy cup. We wish her
Godspeed.

Inside, two children are arguing over something. The
parents make bets on what it is and who is arguing. All
of us lean in to discern which child is screaming, then
one parent stands up with a sigh to mediate. The rest of
us continue the conversation. We talk about work and
family and poll to see which adults are lucky enough
to have children sleeping through the night. We linger
over our plates, which are often paper, and by the time

everyone goes inside, there are LEGOs literally everywhere.

This is what hospitality has become now. A distracted
conversation among parents, commingled with fragmented
points of real connection; a few laughs, and a handful of
time-outs enforced in the corner. Occasionally hospitality is a double date, heels and skinny jeans and beverages
sipped from fancy stemware. We always mean for that to
happen. We talk about it as if it's a legitimate option. But
most of us are still looking for affordable and reliable babysitters and have little to no free time, so frankly we don't
have the luxury of waiting for the perfect conditions to see
each other.

So in the meantime, we make do. We squeeze in
moments of social overlap on Sunday afternoons or in
the paper-thin margin between dinner and bedtimes.
I don't light candles anymore because I'd rather not
turn children into burn victims. And I cook food that is
thoroughly mediocre—lasagna and grilled burgers and
assemble-yourself Cobb salads, because I know I'll be
preparing the meal with 25 percent attention to detail.
The rest of my attention will be appropriated by talking
with people, dispensing snacks to toddlers, and wondering if I remembered to apply mascara to both eyes.

Hospitality didn't always look this frantic. There was
a time I put out cloth napkins and heavy silver napkin
rings, the same ones I received as a wedding gift and
didn't automatically know what they were for. I used

to have food ready the minute everyone was scheduled
to arrive and be infuriated when a single guest was late.
I used to light half a dozen candles all with conflicting
scents, a house aglow and smelling like holiday cin-
namon/floral breeze/French vanilla/pine forest/sugar
cookie.

You could smell how hard I was trying.

And it was terrible.

I used to think hospitality was an event, an occasion
for people to visit the curated trophy room of my life.
See? Our carpets are *so clean*. Did you notice the three
dozen framed photos of our wedding? How *amazing* did
we look? Look! I made something *from this complicated
recipe*. I used the stovetop and oven *at the same time*. Yes,
our bathrooms are *always* this spotless. Why yes, I *do*
wear coordinated shoes and jewelry and makeup in my
own house after 6:00 p.m. Don't you?

I misunderstood hospitality as a means to generate my
own platform, to illuminate it candle by candle. I thought
of it as an elevated place I could stand from and invite
people to gather around and marvel at how well adjusted
I was to adulthood. But eventually, I got tired of it. More
than that, I discovered it didn't really work.

The first dinner party I ever hosted was a failure. It
wasn't that I burned the food or some uninvited guests
arrived or a major kitchen appliance broke. No, I blame
the failure on the cloth napkins. I blame it on the fact
that I poured water out of the Brita dispenser and into a

glass pitcher, then felt authentic regret about forgetting to buy lemons, as if fruit infusion were vitally necessary.

Ultimately, here's why all of that was so terrible: The dinner guests were a handful of single, twenty-something dudes. They were Mike's friends from work, men who drove to our house in beat-up old Broncos and extended-bed pickup trucks and motorcycles that sounded like roaring testosterone. These guys lived with roommates, in houses with sparse and erratic furniture, with kitchens stocked primarily in plastic promotional cups and strawberry Pop-Tarts. They thought they were coming over for dinner, and by "dinner" they meant delivered pizza and beer.

But they arrived to a staged meal that looked strikingly similar to a bridal shower. At the table, they stared at their plates uncomfortably, awkwardly folding and refolding cloth napkins between thumb and forefinger, as if the napkins were ladies' panties they weren't supposed to be touching.

The harder I tried to dazzle, the more uncomfortable everyone became. Mike's friends were not responding well to my attempts to civilize and impress them. They started showing the stiff-necked signs of uneasiness, as though they'd gotten tricked into sophistication. Now, instead of saying yes to more bread, they nodded their heads grimly and said, "Indeed."

Of course, nice food and place settings are beautiful ways to serve guests. But I've come to learn that the first rule of hospitality is the same as the cardinal rule of writing: Consider your audience. Offer food and atmosphere that is helpful and accessible. Make it as easy as possible for guests to feel at home.

Also: Consider paper napkins.

When we still lived in downtown San Diego and before Molly came along, Mike and I devoted the second bedroom of our apartment to an unusual form of hospitality. We became a host house on Couchsurfing.com, a service that allows strangers you meet on the Internet to come and stay with you for free.

I know, I know, it sounds crazy. But at the time we considered this a means to serve tourists coming through our city. The word *hospitality* is actually derived from the same root word as *hospice*, which refers to a resting place for travelers. So in our first year in San Diego, Mike and I thought it would be a meaningful sort of ministry to create an outpost of home for others, a resting place for weary travelers. To act out hospitality in the truest sense of the word.

The first couple we hosted was from Arizona. Online they claimed to be twenty-five-year-olds on a road trip up the California coast. After a week or so of e-mail correspondence and careful inspection of their online profiles, we agreed to host them for a night. Mike and I were very nervous and pretty sure we were making a reckless decision, yet we also felt sure that this was the sort of thing Jesus would have done, serving a stranger without asking anything in return. So we prayed for that sort of bravery and told our parents to stop worrying.

A few days later, when we heard a timid rap on our front door, we opened it to discover that the couch surfers were not who they said they were on the Internet. The couple standing in front of us were not twenty-five-year-olds. They were teenage runaways, pale and lanky, visibly shaking with fear.

Mike and I invited them in and served them spaghetti for dinner. The two of them told stories about homework and their favorite video games and how much they disliked their mothers, not realizing they were inadvertently divulging their age. Both of them were shy and nervous, especially the girl, who told me she liked to read and work at the library after school, a job she loved because she didn't ever have to talk to anyone. The young man was slightly more confident. He occasionally made eye contact with Mike and me and never stopped holding his girlfriend's hand. It was charming, really, how protective he was over his girl, even as a kid himself.

When it came time to go to bed, all four of us were terrified. I'm pretty sure no one slept. But Saturday morning came, and when we met around that rickety table, all of a sudden their story started to tumble out, not because we asked, but because they weren't afraid of us anymore. They had just graduated high school weeks before, and now they wanted to leave home like in the movies. They wanted to have a road trip, to get away.

After we listened, I asked the girl if I could pray with her, and it was super weird and awkward. I couldn't decide if this was the right thing to do or just the most Christian. Needless to say, we prayed without holding hands, and I encouraged her to go home and sort things out with her mom. I sent the couple off with snacks for the road because it felt like the right thing to do for teenagers. And to this day, I still wonder if they turned the car back toward home or kept running away. We never found out.

Obviously after this bizarre experience . . . we decided to keep hosting.

The next couch surfers were two women, both identical to their online representations. One was a yoga teacher from Hawaii, and the other was a psychologist from Arizona. They were best friends on their way to a Buddhist yoga retreat in the mountains of central California. The yoga teacher was everything you would imagine: She wore no makeup, kept her long brown hair in a single braid down her back, and had a voice that was breathy and low, totally Zen. She sat on the floor as we talked, stretching the whole time. The psychologist was slender and tall with glasses. She reminded me of a junior high teacher, chipper and chatty, not in a nervous way, but in an eager, curious way. I gradually realized that both of them were the sort of people who genuinely enjoyed talking to strangers. Soon we learned that both had stayed at other couch surfer homes before, and the psychologist was a host herself. Conversation was effortless and interesting. They told us about their couch surfing experiences, and we told them about our time with the runaways. Then we discussed how to facilitate good conversation with someone you don't know at all, specifically with travelers who stay under your roof.

It was then, almost as if by accident, that the yoga teacher said something that I've never forgotten about hospitality. In her low, earthy voice she said, "I used to think that when people shared a piece of their story with you, they did it because they wanted you to respond with yours, to interject your experience, like an exchange. But now I think that people are really just looking for someone to listen. People need to process out loud and have the space to do it. They don't want someone to hijack their story by telling theirs. So now I try to simply listen, to not hijack other people's stories with my own."

The next morning I walked with the two women downstairs to Starbucks, which I called "our basement." They bought me a coffee as a thank-you, and we exchanged e-mail addresses on a napkin that I have since lost. But the real takeaway of that interaction, for me, was the yoga instructor's astute observation that kept ringing in my ears.

What I thought people wanted from me was input, advice, or collaboration. But seemingly what everyone is really looking for is a listening ear, a no-strings-attached invitation to be at home, to be at rest, to be yourself.

I considered for the first time that I had defined hospitality incorrectly. That what I had done before was really a form of hijacking: inviting people over so I can impress them, asking a question so I can answer too. I molded the accommodation into something that made me look good, using other people's presence to elevate mine. And all of this added up to so much pressure, so much expectation. Instead of serving others, I was auditioning myself before them, and that was the most exhausting part.

We hosted a few more couch surfers after that. Two college-age girls from Germany stayed with us for a week. They were beautiful and bubbly and expressly rule abiding, especially when it came to jaywalking. Later one of them sincerely asked, "So do all Americans have guns in their houses? In Germany, no one has guns. We think America is weird."

A couple of months later Mike and I hosted an advertising copywriter who lived in Philadelphia. I mentioned to him that I was considering writing a book someday, and he suggested I look for writing jobs on Craigslist. I replied that I generally try to avoid job hunting on Craigslist since it's nearly impossible to decipher the difference between legitimate job ads and invitations for murder. To this, he shrugged his shoulders.

The longer we lived in San Diego, the busier we

became and the less we hosted couch surfers, until finally
Mike took our profile down. Hospitality, for us, had
shifted from strangers to people we met in places other
than the Internet, say, church or the dog park. It's as if
we temporarily dated online for friends until we met
some of our own in person.

I got pregnant during our second San Diego year.
And once Molly arrived, hospitality shifted altogether.
Suddenly all our accommodating resources were redirected to a tiny human person, one who needed a crib
and a changing table and one thousand chewable items
that were seemingly everywhere and also nowhere to be
found when needed.

That's the thing about kids: They require every hos-
pitable impulse but filter out motives attached to vanity.
Initially babies seem like a nice little accessory to your
life, something you wear on your chest or bounce on
your hip, a cute mascot in your Christmas photo. That
is, until you realize that wearing them or bouncing them
also means there will be spit-up in your hair, down your
back, or in one unfortunate instance, in your mouth. As
a parent, you serve because you love. You accommodate
because all of a sudden the best possible outcome is not
your own comfort or stability, but your child's. Most of
the time it's not even a deliberate martyrdom, but a sort
of muscle memory you didn't even know you had. If

parenthood has taught me anything, it is that true hospitality is messy and inconvenient. Whether it's with kids or with grown-ups, hospitality is dirty dishes and loud volume and an evening where everyone is pushed past their bedtimes.

But it's also the salve to a burning need.

Because what we need is not more people to impress us or talk over us or serve us food that we don't know how to attack with a fork and knife. There is nothing in me that longs to see what someone else's carpet looks like vacuumed or whether all their serving dishes match. But what I do need is people to show up in my life and testify that I am seen and heard, that I matter. This is why we tackle the dishes and keep the babies up late.

Certainly there is a time for beautiful dinner parties, for place cards and gorgeous centerpieces. Someday soon I hope to sit around a candlelit table of adults having meaningful conversation while luxuriating in the knowledge that all of us found babysitters on the same night. But for now, it's hamburgers on the back patio and diaper changes on the floor and a Frisbee stuck in the tree and two children arguing over whose turn it is to blow bubbles. The best adult conversations will be through text after everyone goes home. But the time together builds a foundation for something more meaningful. Intentional overlap of life makes us safe to one another, so when the big life events come, when we really just need to talk, we know who our people are, who it is we can turn to.

It seems to me, at least in this season of life, that the most essential components of hospitality have nothing to do with the caliber of food or pristine conditions. The most necessary activity is simply the showing up, the choosing to listen, the making a habit of it, even in the mess and in the chaos. It is the adamant, inconvenient act of welcoming people home.

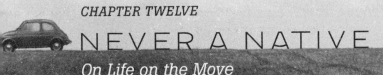

# CHAPTER TWELVE

# NEVER A NATIVE

## *On Life on the Move*

> *Our battered suitcases were piled on the sidewalk again;*
> *we had longer ways to go. But no matter, the road is life.*
> JACK KEROUAC, *On the Road*

Immediately after church on Sundays, we go as a family to the barber. The errand is for Mike, but the barber is right by our church and typically we drive there in one car. So in lieu of an after-church lunch, Mike sits in a swivel chair and describes to his barber exactly how he wants his hair cut while Molly and I plunge into a sea of starvation.

Next to the birth of our children and our own high school romance, I cannot think of any other introduction that has brought Mike as much satisfaction as meeting June, the tiny, middle-aged Vietnamese woman who cuts his hair on Sundays. Both of us love June. She keeps

Mike's hair in trim shape and also protects our marriage from the extensive damage it would surely incur if I were forced to take on the task myself. A few years ago the two of us learned this the hard way, when I walked away offended and Mike walked away partially bald.

One day at the barber, as the clippers buzzed and hummed and wisps of hair somersaulted along the floor, I mindlessly picked up a *Time* magazine that someone else had left behind, silently wishing it were a glossy celebrity magazine or perhaps a sandwich. But I opened it anyway and began skimming the feature article.

The story was about twin astronaut brothers Mark and Scott Kelly, who were about to embark on a year-long study of the physical effects of living in space. One twin would spend a year in orbit. The other would stay here on Earth. NASA would analyze and compare the physical and psychological metrics of each brother. And since twins are outfitted with basically identical biology, one brother could act as the stable control and the other the transient test case.

NASA already knows that the weightlessness of zero gravity has a deteriorating effect on the human body. Former NASA consultant William Evans writes, "While weightlessness seems like everyone's dream of how to maneuver through life without much physical expenditure, it's actually a medical nightmare of gigantic proportions."[31] Without the resistance of gravity, astronauts' hearts weaken because they don't have to work as hard. Bones deteriorate because they don't have to bear the weight of exertion against gravity.[32] This physical atrophy is bad news for NASA, because they want their astronauts to be healthy, obviously. Also, they want to send them to Mars.

From what I understand, the purpose of the twins' NASA study wasn't to peg one living environment against the other—Earth versus space, twin versus twin—but to evaluate how a person can live in either setting and remain healthy. And as I read the article, I couldn't decide which brother I would rather be: the one who gets the roots of stability or the one who gets the wonder of seeing the whole world.

How convenient, I thought, to be able to analyze two diverging roads in real time, to compare the effects of a mobile life with those of a rooted one. Because even though I am not an astronaut, I've occasionally wondered if I, too, experience deterioration from a lack of fixed geography. I've wondered if transience erodes my attention span, my depth of relationship, my muscles of long-term faithfulness. I've wondered if I'm easily disengaged or if I accumulate shallow histories and incomplete tasks, if my friendships are full of untapped potential since many of them are only collocated for a year or two before they migrate to maintenance over the phone. I've wondered if my daughter is a better-adjusted human because of the number of times she's been forced to adjust, if Mike and I are better friends because of the times we have been each other's only friend in a new place.

A life on the move trims our experiences down to the root, time after time, like a weekly haircut. I'm not complaining about it, necessarily. But I have wondered if all this starting over stunts growth or encourages it.

The first six months or maybe a year in a new place are spent making new friends and either memorizing the most efficient route to Chipotle or grieving the absence of one. You might put potted flowers on your porch steps or attach the local grocery store's savings card to your key chain. You find a workout class that you like or a coffee shop that doesn't feel pretentious with excessive industrial decor. There's sometimes a job hunt mixed into this, and a low-grade aggravation at all the ways this new city is markedly different from the last. Simply beginning is such a time-consuming task. But slowly you find some parameters of normal, the loose makings of a routine.

And then, if you've been on the road for a while—if you're in the military or some other vocation that transplants you often and removes the option to stay—within about five minutes of figuring out how to settle in one place, you start wondering about when you'll move away from it. As soon as you adapt to what's in front of you, you start anticipating what's next. It's as if each geographic location is a puzzle to be solved, and once you solve it, the challenge evaporates. When that happens, you're relieved, settled, but you're a little bored, too. So you consider the next round of orders, the next dream, the next challenge, the next location. North Carolina? Japan? Should you stay in the military? Get out? Return home? What was it you heard about the Peace Corps?

For better or for worse, you live suspended between homes in a sort of limbo, feeling homesick or restless or both at the same time. Perhaps a transient life just provides a vocational excuse for an impulse a lot of us already have—to chase down where the greenest grass grows. Whether you live a life that's patently mobile or one that just dreams of being so, I'm convinced there are few things as difficult as remaining present, right where you are.

Call it wanderlust. Call it wayfaring. Call it living free and unfettered. No matter how perfect a home is in the beginning, I'm always surprised by my willingness to leave. After a couple of years, I'm suddenly and predictably ready for something new, hungry to live again in the land of fresh opportunity, the land of new friends, new houses, new everything, where life is either slower or faster—whatever the opposite is of what I have now. I look forward to relying on the GPS to get to the post office and to mispronouncing street names until a local corrects me. I love the excitement of the new frontier, the dreams and possibilities a person can store

in the pockets of an unknown future. I have become
quite good at introducing myself, and I promise I will
help you pronounce my last name after the first syllable
attempt.

So in that final year or last few months in a particular place, here's what I tend to do: I start to make room
in my heart for what's next before we go anywhere at
all. I begin incubating a future that suddenly seems as
though it's running late. I disengage, subtly at first, perhaps by selling furniture on Craigslist—sectional sofas
and end tables that surely won't fit in our next living
room. This next part is hard to admit, but I start to
relationally detach too. I become a less reliable friend
or at least an emotionally distracted one, quietly inching backward from intimacy like a mother dropping
her sensitive child off at day care. I occasionally RSVP
no to events I could probably attend, passively trying
to encourage friends to need me less by meeting fewer
of their needs. It's better for everyone, I tell myself. I'm
making the departure easier, less abrupt.

My friend Suzanne told me that she thinks the mental detachment that occurs before a big move is a sort
of psychological necessity. It's a form of winding down
that may be unavoidable. I mean, ideally, you would
like to be engaged until the very last second, leaning
into the finish line tape. But practically, you're not sure
you can. So you stutter between the right here and the
not yet, living the life in front of you while narrating

it in the past tense. Mentally, you pack your whole life up, but you can't tell if it's in moving boxes or a runaway bag.

On one hand, I congratulate myself as an adventurer, a brave pioneer. But on the other, I consider this: If a third of my time in any location is spent laying roots and a third is spent untangling and uprooting them, then a minority statistic is wedged in between. One third. That's the amount of time I am rooted in a place. And that just doesn't seem like very much time. So I wonder: Am I spending a significant portion of my life detached or suspended or disengaged? Because if I am, it's really important to me to know how to counteract the atrophy of floating.

It seems to me that the lazy expectation of a transient life is that it's easier somehow, as though moving often makes you just slippery enough to evade responsibility. Maybe that is true if you're moving as a perpetual tourist, if you're a consumer and never a contributor, if you vacation nine times a year and hop from job to job only to return home so your mom can do your laundry.

But I think it's possible to be transient and aloof without ever leaving your hometown. I think we can be settled geographically but transient in commitment, in relationship, in purpose. We can be aimless without traveling, passive by nature, reluctant to strain beyond the discomfort required to produce actual growth. This, of course, is not a problem with geography. It is a problem with the roots of the heart. Because where the heart is planted is the same place we dig for treasure.[33]

It's here that I'm reminded that Jesus was a man on the move—"The foxes have holes and the birds of the air have nests, but the Son of Man has nowhere to lay His head."[34] Or to borrow the words of songwriter Rich Mullins, "The hope of the whole world rests / on the shoulders of a homeless man."[35] But while Jesus was nomadic, he didn't wander. He worked within constraints that made his transient ministry strategic. For instance, he met and ministered to thousands of people, yet selected only twelve to be apostles. Then he pared those twelve down to three best friends: Peter, James, and John. He preached to the masses but spent the majority of his time investing in specific people. He was a foreigner on earth, sure, but he wasn't a tourist, a consumer. He traveled as an intentional contributor.

So it seems that even Jesus in his humanity had tethers to accountability, responsibility, and the depth of real relationship. Jesus engaged with humankind, not floating from above, but joining from among. And it is pretty spectacular that as a transcendent figure, he fastened himself to the cumbersome gravity of Earth, to the texture of meaningful relationship. He was anchored to purpose rather than place, and we can be too, but it requires a similar engagement of faith, the cultivation of relationship, and the deep conviction that no place under our feet is wasted.

I believe that a person can also be profoundly rooted in a life on the move. The difference between transience and stability is not necessarily a point of fixed geography, but whether or not someone practices bearing weight where he or she is, whether the roots of the heart have found a place of permanent foundation.

Do you know what astronauts do in space to offset the effects of weightlessness? They work out. For more than two hours a day, they strap themselves to sources of heavy resistance: bicycles and treadmills and weight equipment.[36] Bones and muscles need to be strained daily so they can bear the weight of gravity once they return home. So astronauts make it a priority to hold their bodies accountable to a future life on Earth. They interact with their weightless, temporary environment in a way that mimics the permanent functionality their bodies were made for. Because in order to be a resilient human, you must be durable, and durability is only trained into those who have practiced bearing weight.

Likewise, there is a unique weight to be borne in a transient lifestyle. There are routines of exertion, like exercises, known to those who are never native to the lands they occupy.

For example, living somewhere new will make a

person surer of herself. But before it makes her confident, it will first make her lonely. This can be productive, however, because it's in solitude that you learn the most about yourself and the God who is ever present. That last part instantly gains traction when you're alone. Because the nearness of God sounds like a meaningless platitude until God is a personal friend to you when there are no others.

Independence is another fruit of striking out on your own, but this strength is cultivated through the weight of exertion, say, when you break a major household appliance or your car or a previously reliable tooth. You might carry the budget and all the groceries and a crying baby on one hip, but soon you will also carry a growing conviction that you are far more capable than you ever imagined. You are equipped and purposeful, and suddenly you will notice the curvature of muscle tone in your resilience.

On the road you will collect many friends, a diversity of community unlike anything you expected. But let's not forget the part that comes before: the lack of coherent community, the distance from family, the sheer number of cold introductions necessary to gain momentum. In a new place, there's no guarantee anyone will get your jokes. Often you will have to be the one to initiate conversation, the one to host or cook dinner or ask all the questions. At least half the time it will be very awkward. Unfortunately, you and your guests might not watch the same TV shows, or, heaven forbid, your guests might not watch TV at all. Discussion, then, will have to circle around more technical topics, like how you came to this part of the country or the sort of dishwasher detergent you recommend. But after you press through the effort, the awkward, the cold start, you'll become quite adept at pursuing people. And there are tremendous benefits to being in great shape as an intentional friend.

So it is a sort of consolation, or maybe even a source of deep gratification, that the distinct stresses of a life on the move are the same tensions that train and grow us. I have to remind myself of this often, because frankly it's easy to forget: The effort of transplanting is never wasted. Even if your surroundings seem unaffected by your presence, you are being transformed by the work of growing there.

In John 15, Jesus refers to himself as a vine and you and me as the branches. "Live in me," he says. "Make your home in me just as I do in you."[37] If we do, he promises that we will produce fruit—that is, live rich, productive lives, be helpful to those around us, even fulfill a sense of personal purpose. Essentially, the work of the branches is to live in companionship with Christ, and as a by-product we will enjoy good and abundant life.[38] The greenest grass, the most fruitful branches, it turns out, all spring forth when we are founded securely in the love of God.[39]

But the best life doesn't necessarily mean the lightest

or most carefree. In fact, an impulsive existence can actually be detrimental to the health of the branch, which is why in the same passage Jesus also talks about pruning, the trimming down of branches like regular haircuts for plants. He says that God cultivates us by occasionally clipping at our edges so there's room and reason for us to expand into greater growth. Vines are spreading plants, after all. The branches don't grow up. They grow out. And when they're healthy, when they're pruned, they know how to take new territory and to live well in it.

I'm not saying that a life on the move is for everyone, or that it's better or worse than the more physically rooted kind. But for those of us on the road, I believe that we are sent for a reason, that the challenges are deeply personal and for our good. I believe that God is fostering the fullness of life within us by placing us in contexts that require us to tenaciously remain in him, to strain for what it means to be fully at home.

Most travel experts will tell you that the key to traveling well is to travel light. This is what I remind Mike when we travel somewhere and I consistently forget to pack things like a toothbrush or my driver's license.

But here's the thing about traveling light: Over time, even a mobile life acquires cargo. The first move may fit in the back of a pickup truck, the second might squeeze into a small trailer, but by the third, your life is packed in a semitruck with three bicycles haphazardly strapped to the back.

Our stories are the same way, I think. They become longer, more complex, threaded with greater nuance and context and epiphany as we grow. So, too, we carry our joys, our discoveries, our relationships that act as trophies of victories won. We carry it all, the bitter with the sweet, testimonies that we have lived as fully as we can in every place we have been. We have been pruned and have grown sturdier still. Isn't that sort of a surprise?

A life on the move doesn't necessarily mean a life traveled lightly. But the trials that once seemed unnecessarily heavy are the same tethers that have trained and equipped us, preserving the vitality of the heart by putting it to work. And *it is in the work* that we find proof there is purpose and depth and richness unfolding in every place we are.

Home is sacrificial. It always costs something to build and maintain. One of the mercies, then, of a life of physical transience might be the way it teaches us that home can't really be handed to us. It must be built, labored for, grown into; filled with our stuff; occupied with parts of our history. And maybe that's why the invitation to abide in Christ is so surprising. Because his companionship *is* gifted to us, and as we continue to remain in him, Christ equips us for the work of growing into every place he sends us. In other words, the Permanent One shows us what to do with all these bits of temporary.

What I'm trying to say is that stability is not lost on the road, but trained into us in a different way. And the evidence is in the weight you have felt—the strain of engaging, the loss of leaving, the hopeful trust that growing somewhere new again and again will build something important into you. The goal of a mobile life, then, might not be to travel light, but to respect what you carry.

Because what has challenged you has also preserved you.

You and I on the road? We are strong and getting stronger, filled with breath and purpose and the Spirit of the living God. We are equipped as we cling to him like roots that never give. And if Christ is in us, then we are his ambassadors to the world. And do you know what Jesus' final commission to his followers was?

*Go.*[40]

Go, and carry what is in you, upon you, what you have seen and what you know.

Go, remaining in Christ and growing outward, onward.

Go, creating home from the Home carried within you.

Go, knowing that you are not lost at all, but a found one on the move.

# ACKNOWLEDGMENTS

To Tammy Pal: my mentor, the first reader of this book, and one of the greatest gifts I received from Yuma, Arizona. Thank you for the hours you combed through and prayed over these words. You helped make my writing clearer, vetted my theology until it was sound, and pastored me through the moments it was not. You loved me well and spoke affirmation over me when the task of publicly writing about my personal faith felt crippling. I've told you before that I cannot thank you enough. I still feel that way. I love you.

To Don Pape: Thank you for championing this book and me as a writer in ways that were wholly undeserved.

To Caitlyn: You are a gracious editor and encourager who coached me into clarity and validated my writing voice. I went into publishing expecting a sort of ruthlessness, but the team at NavPress ministered the kindness of Jesus to me over and over again. Thank you.

To the friends I've mentioned in this book and to

those I haven't: Thank you for being a part of our story before it was ever written, for cheering me on when the idea of writing felt risky and absurd.

To the Linns, Andrewses, Hills, Heintzes, and Grassmeyers: You are lifelong friends that span all geography, but also make it *really* hard to live away from Colorado.

To Logan and Kenra: Perhaps no other couple has partnered with us through life changes and spiritual development more than you guys. What a gift you are.

To the Luehmanns, for popping champagne with me on the day I got the book deal, and then again on the day I submitted the manuscript; and also the Vegas and Mireles and Rodríguezes: You all became our San Diego family, and we are so thankful.

To Raquel, for commiserating in the writing, for walking through the deployment and beyond with me, and for reading and reorganizing the homecoming chapter in a way that finally made me write into what I was trying to say: Thank you.

To Zach Betka, for speaking vision into this book at a moment when my clearest thought was *Maybe I should just throw it all away*: You are the brother I inherited far too late in life, but also in the nick of time. I love you.

To the neighborhood park moms/stroller squad: You were everyday friends to me in a season when the tedium of being a stay-at-home mom threatened to swallow me whole. Thanks for meeting me at the park every afternoon and forgiving quickly when Molly went through her robust hitting phase.

To Katie and Kevin DiFelice: Thank you for being the most intentional listeners I have ever known. Your influence is all over these stories, and if there is any wisdom in these pages, I credit much of it to conversations you had with Mike and me during grueling seasons of our lives.

To Mom and Dad: Thank you for sacrificing in a million ways to shape me into the sort of adult who loves Jesus, had the privilege of a great education, and knows how to play the piano. Any talents or strength of character I possess were honed under your instruction, and I am so thankful. I know our family story has had its share of heartache, but the arc of restoration over the past few years has been so beautiful. Pete, you are such a gift to our family and I love you. Linda, you are such a gift to our family and I love you.

Oh, and Mom, thanks for letting me share the story of how you taught me to run. That was the first chapter I drafted—years ago—when this book was just a dream in my heart. But I read it to you at the kitchen table, and you cried and whispered, "Bekah, you must keep writing." That moment changed my life forever.

To Matthew, for making me sharper, smarter, funnier, and more creative: You and I share an intensity that makes us fight ~~sporadically~~ often, but it also produces some of the richest conversations and hardest laughter I have ever known. Only you understand some of the fiery parts of me, because you match and exceed them. I'm so proud to be your sister. I'm so thankful to be your friend.

To Nathan: I can scarcely recall a time before you were a brother to me. You have brought humor, leadership, and wisdom to pivotal moments in our family's story, and I'm so thankful my sister not only married well, but married you.

To Rachel, my first and closest friend: You have borne witness to my entire life and carried me through the hard parts of it. I've always wanted to be more like you. Being mistaken for your twin is one of my greatest accolades. Thank you for going first.

To Molly, the fiery redhead who made me a mom, and to Conrad, the sweet son who arrived just after I finished this book: You two are my greatest joy, my most profound privilege, my hardest work. I love you.

To Mike: Thank you for giving me an adventure to write about and permission to share it. Thank you for calling me a writer before anyone else did, for taking the kids so I could write, for being my best friend, for loving me well. You are my first and true love. I would follow you anywhere.

To Jesus: Thank you for saving me. Thank you for preparing me, equipping me, and bringing to completion every good work, including the writing of this book. Most of all, thank you for expanding and complicating my view of home, and for offering stability of the soul to those, like me, who are prone to wander.

# NOTES

1. Ecclesiastes 3:11.
2. Psalm 139:5; Deuteronomy 31:8.
3. Isaiah 43:19.
4. Exodus 15:20.
5. 2 Samuel 6:14.
6. 1 Kings 18:46.
7. Ephesians 1:4, MSG.
8. Oswald Chambers, "Gracious Uncertainty," in *My Utmost for His Highest* (Grand Rapids, MI: Discovery House, 2010), April 29.
9. Timothy Keller, *The Meaning of Marriage: Facing the Complexities of Commitment with the Wisdom of God* (New York: Penguin, 2013), 111.
10. In the Marine Corps, the hat is called a "cover."
11. PMO stands for "Provost Marshal's Office," which are the military police responsible for security and law enforcement on base.
12. Brené Brown, *Daring Greatly: How the Courage to Be Vulnerable Transforms the Way We Live, Love, Parent, and Lead* (New York: Avery, 2015), 117.
13. John 10:9.
14. "Pasture" = refreshment, security, and satisfaction (see Psalm 23:2; 37:3, NIV).
15. Luke 11:9.
16. 2 Corinthians 10:5, NIV.
17. Ephesians 6:17.
18. Christie Purifoy, *Roots and Sky: A Journey Home in Four Seasons* (Grand Rapids, MI: Revell, 2016), 32.
19. Anne Lamott, *Traveling Mercies: Some Thoughts on Faith* (New York: Pantheon, 1999), 55.

20. John 14:26.
21. 2 Corinthians 5:7.
22. Sarah Bessey, "A Memory of Our True Home," *Sarah Bessey* (blog), October 16, 2014, http://sarahbessey.com/memory-true-home/ (accessed December 15, 2016).
23. Romans 7:19.
24. Isaiah 40:8.
25. 2 Timothy 3:16; the NIV translation says, "All Scripture is God-*breathed*" (emphasis added).
26. 1 Kings 19:10-18.
27. Hebrews 13:5.
28. Frederick Buechner, *Telling the Truth: The Gospel as Tragedy, Comedy, and Fairy Tale* (New York: HarperCollins, 1977), 43.
29. 2 Corinthians 5:5.
30. 2 Corinthians 5:5, MSG.
31. William Evans, *AstroFit: The Astronaut Program for Anti-Aging* (New York: Free Press, 2002), 6.
32. Karen Wright, "Works in Progress: Weightlessness Takes a Heavy Toll on the Health of Our Astronauts," *Discover*, May 2003, http://discovermagazine.com/2003/may/featworks/ (accessed December 16, 2016).
33. Matthew 6:21; Luke 12:34.
34. Matthew 8:20, NASB.
35. Rich Mullins, "You Did Not Have a Home," *The Jesus Record* © 1998, Myrrh.
36. Meredith Popolo, "How Do Astronauts Exercise in Space?" *PC*, July 24, 2013, http://www.pcmag.com/article2/0,2817,2422096,00.asp (accessed December 14, 2016).
37. John 15:4, MSG.
38. John 10:10.
39. Ephesians 3:17.
40. Matthew 28:19.

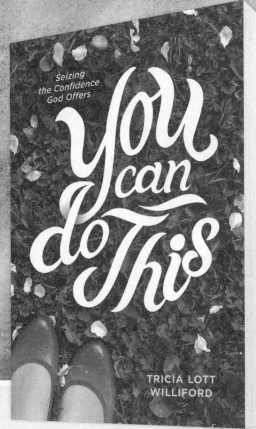